DISCOVERIES
Insights for Church Leadership

BUILDING A HOUSE FOR ALL GOD'S CHILDREN

DIVERSITY LEADERSHIP IN THE CHURCH

JEFFREY S. ROGERS

Abingdon Press
Nashville

BUILDING A HOUSE FOR ALL GOD'S CHILDREN
DIVERSITY LEADERSHIP IN THE CHURCH

Copyright © 2008 by Abingdon Press

This book is printed on acid-free paper.

Library of Congress Cataloging-in-Publication Data

Rogers, Jeffrey S., 1956–
  Building a house for all God's children : diversity leadership in the church / Jeffrey S. Rogers.
    p. cm.
  Includes bibliographical references.
  ISBN 978-0-687-64999-0 (binding: pbk. : alk. paper)
  1. Christian leadership.   2. Multiculturalism—Religious aspects—Christianity.   I. Title.

BV652.1.R64   2008
253—dc22   2008009366

08 09 10 11 12 13 14 15 16 17—10 9 8 7 6 5 4 3 2 1

MANUFACTURED IN THE UNITED STATES OF AMERICA

CONTENTS

PREFACE

This book emerged from the confluence of several streams of experience. My grandparents' families of origin, inhabitants of some of my earliest memories, were Anglican, Lutheran, Mormon, and Roman Catholic. I knew nothing about "religious diversity." They were my family, and I belonged to them all. As a youngster, my view of the world was shaped in a household where Ghanaians, Iranians, and Indians, Christians, Jews, Muslims, and Hindus, immigrants, artists, activists, and anthropologists were welcomed not as "others" but as "us." The capstone of my adolescent "diversity education" occurred the night my family huddled in the back room of our small wood-frame house in the dying days of Jim Crow while a cross burned in our front yard. Later, I epitomized the minority "other" when a professor of African extraction at my historically black *alma mater* took to addressing me in class as "Mr. White Man." Fresh from seminary, I pastored a Baptist church in a rural community where I was a "liberal" born in the despised North; but during my doctoral work, I was dismissed by some as a Southern "conservative." The first half of my life failed to provide me with "a place to come to," in the sense of Robert Penn Warren's resonant phrase, but it gave me a capacity to make in whatever place I came to a home for myself and for others.

That a book emerged, I owe to Calder Ehrmann, Juan, Johnson, R. Roosevelt Thomas, and the inaugural Diversity Leadership Academy of the Richard W. Riley Institute for Government, Politics and Public Leadership at Furman University, where I was introduced to a well-practiced approach to the life I was living. Jim Pitts gave me the opportunity to produce the core of this book as lectures for the Furman Pastor's School. The faculty and administration of Gardner-Webb University provided the catalyst for pulling it all together as lectures and a sermon on unity and diversity in the university. Still, it would have stayed in the filing cabinet if not for Abingdon's Robert Ratcliff who saw a book in it and made it happen. Lurking behind it is the persistence of Charles Kimball, who goaded me out of the insular existence of a scholar writing for other scholars into the public arena.

I am incalculably indebted to the congregation and staff of First Baptist Greenville, both for building a house where my family and I are welcome and for their extraordinary patience and encouragement. To everyone whose stories are part of my story and mine of theirs, I am grateful. To Bev, for thirty years and counting, to Marshall, Graham, and Heath, Mack, Mason, Naomi, Sarah, Alex, Sarah, Jodiannah, Olivia, and all God's children everywhere, this is for you with my hope and prayer that the church will always be, with Robert Frost, a " 'place where, when you have to go there, they have to take you in. . . . Something you somehow haven't to deserve.' "

Lent 2008
Greenville, South Carolina

CHAPTER 1

A DIVERSE NEW WORLD—AND OLD

"The way I see it," said the dentist, "we're all climbing the same mountain. We're just taking different paths up the side. What's wrong with looking at it that way?" Before I could respond, a young woman standing behind me exclaimed, "What's wrong? I'll tell you what's wrong. Jesus is the *only* way! There's no mountain, there aren't any paths, there's only one way, and it's Jesus." As I stood between these two members of the congregation I serve, I recalled Lyle Schaller's observation in *The New Context for Ministry*: "From a pastoral perspective, the most difficult assignment is to serve a theologically pluralistic congregation that also includes great diversity in the level of Christian commitment."[1] Diversity is more expensive than homogeneity, Schaller says, and at that moment the three of us were experiencing one of its intangible but real costs.[2]

On the face of it, this Sunday-evening encounter reflected the familiar tension between the theological perspectives of "pluralism" and "exclusivism."[3] But beneath the surface of this exchange were other powerful currents of diversity. There were diversities of generation, gender, faith-development, family dynamics, personality type, spirituality type, and congregational connectedness, to name the most obvious ones. These two committed Christians also had

1

diverse expectations of me, their pastor, to whom they had come for conversation. Instead, they found themselves in a pointed exchange with each other.

Novelist Cassandra King's engaging exposé of the pastoral household and vocation, *The Sunday Wife*, captures another minister in a diversity tangle. The Reverend Dr. Ben Lynch arrives late on a Sunday evening at the beachfront home of his parishioners Maddox and Augusta Holderfield, who have befriended his wife, Dean, the title character of the novel. After reprising his sermon on Jesus' walking on the water that the three vacationers had missed, Lynch says:

> "Preaching about the miracles in the Bible can be like walking a tightwire." "How so?" Maddox asked. Ben shrugged. "You know. Some folks are strict literalists when it comes to the Word of God. Others—like you two, I'm sure"—he nodded toward Augusta and Maddox—"are uncomfortable with the idea of miracles." "Wait a minute, Dr. Lynch," Augusta said. "You're making an assumption, aren't you? I believe in the Virgin Birth. I believe Jesus turned water to wine, and have no doubt that He walked on water and calmed the seas. And I certainly believe He arose from the dead." . . . "Oh," he said lamely, then chuckled. "Nowadays, it's unusual for people to think that way. In this modern age . . ." He shrugged, letting the idea drop, and looked to Maddox for help. Maddox leaned back in the rocker. "Miracles in our modern age. Fascinating subject, isn't it? What do you think, Ben?" "Me? Well . . ." He rubbed his hands together and frowned, as though deep in thought. "To tell you the truth, Maddox, I have no problem with whatever theory my parishioners embrace. I can relate to both literalists and the skeptics." Augusta gave a whistle. "If you ever give up preaching, you could go into politics."[4]

Confronted with theological diversity in his congregation, Ben Lynch chose to straddle the fence. But as Augusta Holderfield's reaction to his evasiveness indicates, equivocation—fence straddling—will not suffice in a church composed of diverse constituencies who expect authenticity and integrity rather than political expedience from their leaders.

Obviously, pastors are not alone in facing the challenges of diversity in the church. A six-year-old finished his Mother's Day card, turned to a teacher in his Sunday school class, and asked for another sheet of construction paper.

"No, Marcus," she said nicely. "Now that you are finished, you can go over to the rug for the Bible story. We'll start as soon as everyone else is done."

"But I need to do another one," he insisted.

"Why?" she asked. "This one is very nice. I'm sure your mother will love it."

"But I need to make one for my other mommy."

As the woman stood with a slightly quizzical look on her face, another teacher in the room stepped in with a fresh piece of construction paper in hand. "Yes, you do, Marcus. Here you are. If you don't get this one done before we start the story, you can listen in from over here while you finish it." She turned to the other teacher and said with a smile, "I'll fill you in later." While preparing the Sunday school craft for the day, no one had anticipated that one youngster in the class would need to make a Mother's Day card to take home to both of his mommies. To deal wisely and well with the diversity in and around the church today, pastors, staff, and congregational leaders need a framework for understanding diversity that few congregational settings currently exhibit.

DIVERSITY: A NEW ISSUE, AN OLD ISSUE

"Diversity as an issue is new," R. Roosevelt Thomas Jr. wrote in 1991.[5] The founder of the American Institute for Managing Diversity and a leading expert in the burgeoning field of diversity management, Thomas identified three turbulent forces buffeting American businesses and institutions: global competition, changing demographics, and an increasing reluctance of individuals to assimilate or "fit in" by shedding their identities. In *Beyond Race and Gender*, he included the following scenario as an example of an emerging "diversity tension."

A new suburban church, founded as a nondenominational organization, attracted members from a variety of denominations. For a time, there was harmony. But before long, individual members began to push for traditions and practices that they had experienced in their own denominations. The various practices were at odds with each other, and with the nondenominational concept. Some members felt that the church had tilted too much toward one particular denomination. In the resulting tension, many members left the church.[6]

Individuals "switching" churches—and denominations and nondenominations—has contributed to a new degree of diversity in local congregations, as Wade Clark Roof and William McKinney documented in *American Mainline Religion: Its Changing Shape and Future*. Roof and McKinney identified an increasing "internal institutional pluralism" in local congregations now beset by "diversity in ideas and styles, changing definitions of common beliefs . . . and fluidity in personal commitment and organizational structures."[7] Roof subsequently collaborated with Jackson W. Carroll to explore the shape of generational diversity—preboomer, baby boomer, and generation X—in local congregations in *Bridging Divided Worlds*. Their research explores how these three generations form distinct cohorts in the church with varying values, views, beliefs, practices, spiritual styles, priorities in the church, and ways of relating to organized religion and to one another. Carroll and Roof depict the swirling mixture of diversity currents when they suggest that a local congregation

> represents a thick mix of world views, values, symbols, meanings, and practices that participants bring to them. Gender, ethnic, lifestyle, regional and social class distinctions are among the most important that are reflected in a single congregation's gathering. The mix also includes generational difference as members of a cohort bring their experiences and expectations to the congregation. This diverse combination of perspectives is often cross-cutting and cross-pressuring,

creating a complex set of popular undercurrents beneath the congregation's surface.[8]

From a wider angle of vision, Robert Wuthnow charted the transformation of spirituality in America since the 1950s with the emergence of a new spiritual freedom that has significantly expanded the theological diversity of local congregations as well as American culture at large.[9]

At the same time, another powerful diversity current has emerged in and around the church in the form of "identity politics." The late William Sloane Coffin sounded the following warning in *A Passion for the Possible: A Message to U.S. Churches*:

> The challenge today is to seek a unity that celebrates diversity, to unite the particular with the universal, to recognize the need for roots while insisting that the point of roots is to put forth branches. What is intolerable is for difference to become idolatrous. When absolutized, nationalism, ethnicity, race, and gender are reactionary impulses. They become pseudoreligions, brittle and small, without the power to make people great. No human being's identity is exhausted by his or her gender, race, ethnic origin, or national loyalty. Human beings are fully human only when they find the universal in the particular, when they recognize that all people have more in common than they have in conflict, and that it is precisely when what they have in conflict seems overriding that what they have in common needs most to be affirmed.[10]

In contrast to Coffin's call for affirming what human beings have in common, combatants in the current "culture wars" raging around and within the church frequently absolutize attributes and then lionize or demonize persons on the basis of those attributes.

Coffin's warning, Thomas's scenario, and the analyses of Roof and McKinney and Carroll and Wuthnow are all grounded in the contemporary American religious landscape, but the tension and turbulence of "internal institutional pluralism"—diversity—is as old as the church itself. The following scenario in a local congregation predates Thomas's example by more than 1,900 years.

> A new congregation is started by a church planter in an unchurched environment. For a time, a clear sense of identity and unity prevails as the perspectives of its founder continue to inform the group's theology and worship. Before long, other Christian teachers pass through, and individual members begin to push for the adoption of practices commended by these teachers. The congregation's theology, worship and identity start to shift. In the resulting tension, its founder writes an angry letter accusing the church of "turning to a different gospel." (Galatians 1:6)

The apostle Paul's Letter to the Galatians reflects a bitter controversy in the early church that is a clear indication of the antiquity of diversity tensions in local congregations. A critical fault line in this dispute that featured Paul on one side and Peter and James on the other (according to Paul in Galatians 2:11-14) can be traced in part to their respective communities of origin: Paul in a Hellenistic Judaism of the Diaspora and Peter and James in a more insular and conservative Palestinian Judaism. In a sense, each "began to push for traditions and practices" closer to what "they had experienced in their own denominations."

Diversity-driven tension is probably as old as religious practice itself. The story of Cain and Abel in Genesis 4 is often interpreted sociologically as reflecting the ancient cultural conflict between herders (Abel) and farmers (Cain). But the flash point of the tension in the story arises not from the two brothers' occupations but from their differing religious experiences and perceptions.

> In the course of time Cain brought to the LORD an offering of the fruit of the ground, and Abel for his part brought of the firstlings of his flock, their fat portions. And the LORD had regard for Abel and his offering, but for Cain and his offering

he had no regard. So Cain was very angry, and his countenance fell. . . . And when they were in the field, Cain rose up against his brother Abel, and killed him. (Genesis 4:3-5, 8)

Interpreters have long haggled over the reason for the divine preference for one offering over the other. The great medieval Jewish commentator Rashi favored the interpretation that Cain offered *"inferior* [fruits]" of the ground, in particular mere "flax seed."[11] Martin Luther preferred to locate the problem not in the offering but in the person who offered it. Luther wrote:

> When Moses says: "The Lord had regard for Abel and his offering," does he not clearly indicate that God is wont to look at the individual rather than at the work, to see what sort of individual he is? If, then, the individual is good, his work also pleases Him; but if the individual is not good, his work displeases Him.[12]

In whatever manner the divine preference is parsed, the two characters in the story became trapped in a religious diversity tension that eventually exploded in murderous rage. It is an ancient narrative with a perpetually contemporary plot.

DIVERSITY: A NEW CONTEXT, AN OLD CONTEXT

As Charles Kimball has pointed out in *When Religion Becomes Evil,* "the world has always been religiously diverse," but in the aftermath of the events of September 11, 2001, there is a new urgency to our encounter with that diversity. Kimball writes: "The challenges posed by religious diversity combined with the inescapable fact of global interdependence are now as clear as the September sky over New York that fateful day."[13] Quite understandably, in the post-9/11 context the global issues have attracted most of the attention, but "the turbulent forces connected with religion in our world"[14] are every bit as local as they are global, and they are Christian as well as Muslim.

In May of 1997, a member of the South Carolina Board of Education was speaking to a group of concerned citizens in Anderson, South Carolina, about his proposal that the Ten Commandments should be displayed in every public school classroom. He argued that doing so would promote discipline in the schools and family values in society. When he was asked how Buddhist and Muslim children might feel about his proposal, he responded, "Screw the Buddhists and kill the Muslims." Evidently the irony was lost on him that it is a rather odd defense of the Ten Commandments that endorses rape and murder. Those who rallied to his support by suggesting that he had simply articulated publicly the way many Christians feel privately missed both the irony and one of the most important lessons of early twentieth-century European history: hate speech directed at religious minorities by officials of the state is a harbinger of fascism. Hate speech and hate crimes alike illustrate the extreme to which some people in religious communities will go "when faiths collide," in the expression of the esteemed historian of American religion Martin Marty.[15]

Diana Eck's Harvard-based "Pluralism Project" has documented the fact that "the United States has become the most religiously diverse nation on the earth."[16] In the last three decades of the twentieth century, she writes:

> [M]assive movements of people both as migrants and refugees have reshaped the demographics of our world. . . . But nowhere, even in today's world of mass migrations, is the sheer range of religious faith as wide as it is today in the United States. . . . This is an astonishing new reality. We have never been here before.[17]

What were once called "world religions" are now "American religions." Our neighbors are Baha'is, Buddhists, Hindus, Jains, Muslims, Sikhs, and Zoroastrians, to name only a few. "Religious diversity," Eck writes, "is an observable fact of American life today."[18] This burgeoning religious diversity of American communities has created a challenging new context of diversity for local congregations and their leadership.

It is quite correct to say of the American religious landscape, "This is an astonishing new reality. We have never been here before." But it is also true that in the history of Christian faith and belief this reality is neither all that new, nor is this territory entirely unfamiliar. Christian theology and practice have centuries of experience with contexts characterized by religious diversity. After all, Christian faith and belief were born on the continent of Asia and are as old in Africa as they are in Europe. Christian faith and practice flourished in Syria and Turkey and Algeria and Tunisia before becoming ascendant in Rome or arriving in Geneva. Christian practice and theology are no strangers to a context characterized by diversities of all kinds.

The same is true of Christian Scripture. The fact that "the world has always been religiously diverse" is reflected throughout the Bible. According to the book of Genesis, the families of Abraham and Sarah, the biblical ancestors of Judaism, Christianity, and Islam, originated in "Ur of the Chaldees" in southern Babylonia, modern-day Iraq (Genesis 11:28-31). They migrated north to Haran in Syria, Genesis says, before they set out south, traveled to Egypt, and returned to live in Canaan. Scripture tells us, then, that the ancestors of Israel—and the church—were ancient Iraqi families who wandered the length of the Fertile Crescent. No strangers to diversity, these.

Moses, the Bible tells us, was born and reared in Egypt, a land of ancient and mysterious gods and diverse customs. Scholars and dilettantes alike have long speculated about what of Egyptian origin Moses brought into the faith and practice of his band of Palestinian refugees. As an adult, Moses fled Egypt, we are told, and married Zipporah, one of seven daughters of Jethro, a Midianite priest (Exodus 18). According to the book of Exodus, then, the revered founder of ancient Israelite religion and the framer of Old Testament law (including the Ten Commandments!) pioneered biblical faith and practice in the context of an interfaith marriage. No stranger to diversity, he.

Jesus of Nazareth was born into a Palestine rocked by divisions among Jews struggling with one another to define the form and content of faithful Jewish living in a cultural context infused with Roman, Hellenistic, and Persian influences. According to the Gospels, Jesus' ministry brought him into contact not only with representatives of diverse streams of Judaism such as Pharisees, Sadducees, Samaritans, and (no doubt) Essenes, but also with a Gerasene swineherd, Roman centurions, a Syro-Phoenician woman, and a Roman procurator. Jesus of Nazareth was no stranger to diversity.

Clearly, the Old and New Testaments derive from a richly diverse context. Elements of ancient Canaanite, Egyptian, Mesopotamian, and Persian religions are present in the Old Testament, and the New Testament reflects them also, along with Hellenistic and Roman religion and occasional indigenous belief and practice. The Bible was written in and for a culturally and religiously diverse world. If the biblical witness and the testimony of the early history of the Christian church are any indication, diversity is neither new nor a threat to Christian faith and belief. To the contrary, diversity characterizes the historical, cultural, and religious matrix in which Christian faith and belief were born, were nurtured, and first flourished.

Diversity, then, is both a new issue in the church and an old one; both a new context for the church and an old one. For local congregations to respond effectively to the internal and external diversity they face, leadership with both vision and expertise is a necessity.

DIVERSITY LEADERSHIP: VISION

In *Leading Change*, John P. Kotter writes: "*Vision* refers to a picture of the future with some implicit or explicit commentary on why people should strive to create that future." Vision is "a central component of all great leadership."[19] No one has done energizing vision any better than Walter

Brueggemann in *The Prophetic Imagination*, a classic of twentieth-century American biblical theology. Brueggemann reads the prophets of the Old Testament in relation to "the contemporary situation of the church."[20] He characterizes the theological reflection evident in the prophetic literature—and therefore to be emulated in the church—this way:

> No prophet ever sees things under the aspect of eternity. It is always partisan theology, always for the moment, always for the concrete community, satisfied to see only a piece of it all and to speak out of that at the risk of contradicting the rest of it. Empires prefer systematic theologians who see it all, who understand both sides, and who regard polemics as unworthy of God and divisive of the public good.[21]

Brueggemann's polarities are clear and compelling: prophets *versus* systematic theologians, alternative communities *versus* the dominant culture. Authentic prophetic ministry in the church is equated with partisanship and polemics, while understanding both sides and eschewing divisiveness is a sellout. More than a quarter century later, partisanship, polemics, and divisiveness rule in the church and in the dominant culture alike, as both have become caught up in literal and figurative wars, including the war on terror, the war in Iraq, culture wars, gender wars, mommy wars, and worship wars. After decades of vision energized by the partial, the partisan, and the polemical, it is time for the prophetically inclined to refocus their vision and redirect their energy.

In a delightful and irascible little book titled *The Art of Humane Education*, Donald Phillip Verene commends the ancient rhetorical virtue of eloquence, "which refers not to fine phraseology but to the *speech that captures the whole of a subject.* . . . The speech of the part is fixed, often propositional, descriptive, and argumentative. It focuses the mind's eye to see as if by lamplight in the dark. Eloquent speech proceeds as if by sunlight, even if its seeing is incomplete."[22] Eloquence, says Verene, is "*to speak on the whole of the subject and is thus wisdom speaking."*[23] This distinction between the speech of the part—prophetic speech—and speaking of the whole—wisdom speaking—is a reminder to the church that the "prophetic imagination" is not the only biblical imagination to which to turn for vision and energy. The wisdom tradition—irenic and international in perspective—speaks in an entirely different tone and timber than the prophetic tradition, and it sees from a different angle of vision on God, the world, and humankind. When it draws on the prophetic tradition, the proclamation of the gospel as partiality *for* some and *against* others is "lamplight in the dark." When the proclamation of the gospel operates in a wisdom mode, it is "sunlight" shining on a field of wheat and weeds that "grow together until the harvest" (Matthew 13:30), consistent with the intent of the Creator who makes the "sun rise on the evil and on the good, and sends rain on the righteous and on the unrighteous" (Matthew 5:45). The hopelessly utopian vision of an alternative community purged of the taint of the dominant culture is essentially partial, unlike wisdom's eloquent counsel that eliminating the weeds "would uproot the wheat along with them" (Matthew 13:29).

Sadly, the picture of a homogeneous, theologically and politically purged alternative community is the only future that prophetic polemicists on the left and on the right offer today's church. Their respective visions do not embrace diversity in the church; they eliminate it. Authentic diversity leadership in local congregations will require an energizing vision that is grounded elsewhere than in prophetically styled partisanship that results in partiality and polarization rather than in reconciliation and redemption. As local congregations attempt to address the challenges presented by the literal and figurative wars raging around them and within them, a new energizing vision is necessary, as are new strategies and tactics for churches to speak wisdom to an increasingly foolish and fractured world in which it is impossible to pull out the weeds without uprooting the wheat also. Partiality, partisanship, and polemics masquerading as prophetic witness will no longer do. The energizing vision for our time must be to build a house for *all* God's children, not just for some; an enterprise that will require a new breed of "diversity leadership" in the church.

DIVERSITY LEADERSHIP: EXPERTISE

In order to live into a new vision, local congregations and their leaders must develop new expertise—new ways of seeing, thinking, believing, and behaving—to respond wisely and well to the variety of diversities they are encountering. The first step in the direction of this expertise is a new, more comprehensive definition of diversity, and the second step is the cultivation of a more "eloquent" theological framework than the partiality and polemics provided by "prophetic proclamation." In *Building a House for Diversity*, R. Roosevelt Thomas Jr. points to the inadequacy of the conventional understanding of diversity, which emphasizes incorporating a discrete set of "others" into a preexisting "main" group. "In this traditional view," writes Thomas, "it is the 'others' who constitute the diversity."[24] This essentially partial and ultimately polarizing perspective has given rise to responses to diversity such as "affirmative action" and "inclusion," both of which associate "diversity" with the "others" who are incorporated into the "main." According to Thomas, there is a widespread "confusion between diversity and inclusion." Inclusion, he writes, "is an exercise in arithmetic."[25] It is a tinkering with representation and demographics in which the burden of diversity is always carried by persons identifiable as "others," who are championed by some, loathed by others, and ignored by most. In contrast to the conventional view, Thomas defines diversity as "any significant collective mixture that contains similarities as well as differences."[26] He writes:

> Once we begin to see diversity as *the total collective mixture*, made up of the "main" and also the "others," it becomes obvious that diversity is not a function of race or gender or any

other us-versus-them dyad, but *a complex and ever-changing blend of attributes, behaviors, and talents.*[27]

Thomas's definition is clearly more "eloquent" than the traditional understanding of diversity in that it insists on speaking to "the whole of the subject"—*the total collective mixture.* His definition sheds sunlight rather than lamplight on diversity because diversity includes similarities as well as differences and because no particular differences are spotlighted while others remain in darkness. Once the focus shifts from "us-versus-them dyads" such as race, gender, denomination, sexual orientation, and so on, to the total collective mixture in a congregation, leaders are able to proceed by asking questions instead of by making arguments. In an assertion about philosophy and education that is equally true of theology and the church, Verene insists:

> [A]rgument can never settle anything. Despite this defect of argument—that for every argument there is always a good counterargument—we should not become enemies of argument. In intellectual exchange argument can serve to bring out the features of a claim. But in our time argument . . . has become an intellectual fetish.[28]

Says Verene: "Argument is always a partial way of thinking. . . . Arguments are never in themselves wisdom. . . . In the place of argument as the leading form of instruction I would put the question as the fundamental device."[29] Diversity leadership in the church proceeds by asking questions instead of making arguments. Thomas puts these questions at the outset:

> What is the [church's] vision?
> Its mission?
> Its principal objectives?
> Its key strategies?
> Do we need diversity in this organization (or in this situation)?

If so, what kind?
If so, how much?[30]

In speaking of the whole instead of the parts, the question is, What is the *complex and ever-changing blend of attributes, behaviors, and talents* in this congregation? Equipped with a new definition of diversity and beginning with *questions* of diversity instead of with an argument for or against it, leaders in the church can begin to understand diversity differently and respond to it more wisely.

There is, of course, a critical distinction to be drawn between Thomas's settings of business and industry and the context of the church. Dealing with diversity in the church must be grounded in an understanding of "ultimate concern" as well as political, social, and economic concerns.[31] In other words, diversity leadership in the church necessarily entails an appropriate theological framework along with an adequate definition of diversity. Once again, the lines of conversation are both old and new.

In the internally and externally diverse setting of the early centuries of the church, Christian theologians faced major doctrinal and apologetic challenges in trying to explain the diverse manifestations of God in Scripture and the church's experience. How is the God who is spoken of as parent—as in "Father" in Matthew 5:16—also the offspring of the parent—as in "my Son" in Matthew 3:17? How is God who is spoken of as "spirit" (John 4:24) whom "no one has ever seen" (1 John 4:12) also God who "became flesh and lived among us" (John 1:14)? Stung by charges of polytheism from outside the church and rankled by radically divergent teaching inside the church, early Christian theologians settled on the doctrine of the Trinity as a vehicle for articulating the coherence of the diversity of the divine self-revelation. Simply stated, though by no means simple, the doctrine of the Trinity asserts, "The Father is God, the Son is God, and the Holy Spirit is God, and yet there are not three Gods but one God." Given the internal and external controversies and the philosophical categories of the second through the sixth centuries that shaped the development of the doctrine of the Trinity, it is no wonder that the prevailing emphasis of trinitarian reflection has been on the *oneness* of the three, the *unity* of the Godhead. Unfortunately, largely lost in the church's quest for unity, consistency, and stability is the recognition that the Trinity is every bit as much a doctrine of the diversity of God as it is a doctrine of the unity of God. As Diana Eck observes, "[A]ll the great monotheisms, however unitary they may seem from a distance, become more complex the closer we get," and the Trinity is an expression of "the many-sidedness of our symbolic expressions of Ultimate Reality."[32]

In the early 1980s, the German theologian Jürgen Moltmann suggested in *The Trinity and the Kingdom* that the Trinity is more than a doctrine of "individual persons." It is a doctrine of "person with person" or a doctrine of community.[33] Long before—and long after—Western Christianity began doing theology under the influence of Augustine, who turned the Trinity into a psychological doctrine, Eastern Christianity subscribed to a *social* doctrine of the Trinity. The Trinity as a doctrine of community plays a far more dynamic role in the church and the world than the Trinity as a doctrine of persons. For example, in the fourteenth century, a Russian named Bartholomew Karillovich, who has come to be known in history and legend as Saint Sergius of Radonezh, founded a monastery in Moscow dedicated to the Holy Trinity. Saint Sergius's goal, according to a fifteenth-century account, was "so that 'contemplation of the Holy Trinity would conquer the hateful fear of this world's dissensions.'"[34] His confidence in the dissension-conquering capacity of the Trinity was not merely theological lip service, as Saint Sergius is remembered for more than contemplation. He was a strong supporter and principal motivator of a Russian prince named Dmitry Donskoy, who pursued a policy of unification that brought the independent and infighting local Russian principalities together and led them in

September of 1380 to the first significant Russian military victory against the Mongols. Conquering "the hateful fear of this world's dissensions" by uniting the infighting and overcoming the oppressors was an essentially theological pursuit for Saint Sergius, who was motivated by a distinctively Eastern understanding of the Trinity: "Being undivided, the Trinity denounced strife and called for togetherness; being individualized, it condemned oppression and called for liberation."[35] This dynamic, social understanding of the Trinity—denouncing strife and calling for togetherness, and condemning oppression and calling for liberation—models for the church in every time and place both unity in diversity and diversity in unity.

Fascinatingly, a similarly dynamic understanding appears to underlie the apostle Paul's threefold benediction in 2 Corinthians 13:13: "The grace of the Lord Jesus Christ, the love of God, and the communion of the Holy Spirit be with all of you." Interpreters of 2 Corinthians have frequently noted the sharp contrast between the personal, unifying tone of 13:11-13 and the preceding content of this letter to the church in Corinth as we have it in its present form. For example, in chapter 11, Paul claims accusingly that some who have come to the Corinthian church have proclaimed "another Jesus" than the one Paul had preached when he was there. In chapter 12, Paul expresses concern that there is "quarreling, jealousy, anger, selfishness, slander, gossip, conceit, and disorder" in the Corinthian congregation. As chapter 13 nears its conclusion, Paul speaks threateningly of the prospect that when he returns to Corinth he might "have to be severe in using the authority that the Lord has given [him] for building up and not for tearing down" (13:10). All is clearly not well in the Corinthian congregation, nor are things well between Paul and the Corinthians. And it is at precisely this unwell and threatening juncture that we arrive in 2 Corinthians 13:13 at what later commentators will call a "trinitarian formula." It is as though Paul somehow believed that such contemplation could conquer the hateful fear of the Corinthians' dissensions and the dissension between the Corinthians and Paul.

What the apostle Paul and Saint Sergius of Radonezh can teach us about the Trinity is that as goes the Trinity, so goes the church. The doctrine of the Trinity is a both/and assertion of the diversity in unity and the unity in diversity of the very Being of God in God's own self as well as in God's self-revelation in the world. And to the degree that the Christian community is what Paul calls "one body in Christ," we are both many and at the same time one, in terms that sound suspiciously similar to those that Christian theologians will use in their formulations of the Trinity: "We, who are many, are one body in Christ, and individually we are members one of another" (Romans 12:5). We are both individuals and at the same time members of one another. As a social doctrine, the Trinity is not just about who God is. The Trinity is also every bit as much about who we are. Embracing the diversity of God—as well as the unity of God—is an indispensable step in the direction of theological expertise in a church whose vibrant variety reflects the God whom it worships and serves.

Embracing the diversity of Scripture is another indispensable step. In an effort to "speak on the whole of the subject" rather than only a part, the next three chapters will explore seven biblical responses to diversity that are evident in the Old and New Testaments.

STRADDLING THE FENCE —OR LEAPING IT

A Sermon on 1 Corinthians 8

Sometimes I lie awake at night. I lie awake at night wondering if even the grace and power of God are sufficient to hold us together. I serve a local congregation whose mission statement includes the sentence, "We believe in the authority of the Bible, the equality of all members, unity in diversity, and the priesthood of all believers." In the history of the Christian church, we have extensive experience wrestling with "the authority of the Bible" and "the priesthood of all believers." But "equality of all members" and "unity in diversity" are decidedly minority opinions in the church's long and storied past. Down through the centuries, the church has more often opted for hierarchy than for equality, and it has frequently opted for unity by homogeneity rather than "in diversity." "Unity in diversity" and "equality of all members" are challenging articulations of the nature of Christian community that are neither all that widely storied nor all that extensively lived out in the church.

As in many other congregations, there are multiple diversities evident in the congregation I serve. Individuals among our number believe in and stand for many, many different things. We actively disagree with one another on matters theological, social, political, economic, aesthetic, and athletic, to name only a few. We remind me sometimes of the story of a synagogue in Eastern Europe when the *Shemaʿ* was recited. Half the congregation, it is said, stood up for the recitation, and half remained sitting. Not only that, but the half that was seated yelled at those who were standing to sit down, and the ones who were standing yelled at the half that was sitting to stand up. A new rabbi, learned though he was in the law and commentaries, had no idea how to avert the chaos that broke out every time the *Shema* was recited. Finally, he decided to consult one of the founders of the synagogue, a homebound ninety-eight-year-old man. The rabbi went to the elderly man's home and took with him representatives of the two warring factions. The one whose compatriots stood during the *Shema* said to the old man, "Is it our tradition to stand during the *Shema*?"

"No, that is not our tradition," answered the old man.

"See!" said the one whose compadres sat. "So it is our tradition to sit during the *Shema*?"

"No," the old man responded, "that is not our tradition."

Whereupon the rabbi said to him, "But every time we recite the *Shema*, half stand and half sit and they yell at each other about whether we should . . ."

"Ah," interrupted the old man, "that's our tradition!"

Some of us actively supported the adoption and expansion of the North American Free Trade Agreement, while others were among our nation's most vocal and active opponents of NAFTA. Some of us were strong and public advocates of our nation's invasion and continuing military presence in Iraq, while others of us opposed it from the beginning. Some of us are watching the legal and political debates over same-sex marriage with horror because we interpret them as a sign of our nation's moral decline. Others of us, however, are watching those same debates with great hope because of what the expansion of the legal rights and protections of marriage would mean for our children, our friends, or ourselves. I confess that sometimes I lie awake at night wondering if even the grace and power of God are sufficient to hold us together.

And yet I am convinced that our highest and most noble calling as a community of believers is to be a living model here and now of God's coming and peaceable diversity-in-unity kingdom in which, according to the prophet Isaiah:

The wolf shall live with the lamb,
  the leopard shall lie down with the kid,
the calf and the lion [shall feed] together,
  and a little child shall lead them.
The cow and the bear shall graze,
  their young shall lie down together;
  and the lion shall eat straw like the ox.
The nursing child shall play over the hole of the asp,
  and the weaned child shall put its hand on the adder's den.
They will not hurt or destroy
  on all my holy mountain;
for the earth will be full of the knowledge of the LORD
  as the waters cover the sea. (Isaiah 11:6-9)[1]

This beatific vision of Isaiah makes it clear that "diversity in unity" is not unity by homogeneity. It's wolves and lambs—without having to replace the lambs periodically. It's leopards and kids, calves and "lions, and tigers, and bears, oh my!" Isaiah's vision offers us a picture of a future community composed of former predators and former prey, former perpetrators and former victims, former terrorizers and former terrorized. It's not a kingdom cleansed by the expulsion or elimination of one by the other. It's a kingdom created by the incorporation of them all together. Sometimes I lie awake wondering.

In his correspondence with the young and overly enthusiastic church in the cosmopolitan city of Corinth, the apostle Paul found it necessary to respond to multiple challenges to the Corinthian congregation's unity. I suspect that sometimes the apostle Paul lay awake at night wondering if even the grace and power of God were sufficient to hold the church in Corinth together. In a moment of pastoral transparency he confessed to the Corinthians, "I am under daily pressure because of my anxiety for all the churches" (2 Corinthians 11:28). Been there, done that, got the T-shirt.

In the eighth chapter of 1 Corinthians, Paul addressed a question that threatened to divide the church: Is it permissible or appropriate for Christians to eat meat that has been sacrificed to idols? By way of background, we should understand that in the urban centers of the ancient world, the temples were the butcher shops. The nearly exclusive source of meat in the diet of people who lived in Corinth would have been the sanctuaries of pagan deities. That being the case, for some members of the church in Corinth, procuring protein for their family's diet presented them with a crisis of conscience, a theological conundrum, and an ethical dilemma, because the only meat available to them came from the sacrificial system of a pagan cult. So to eat or not to eat meat was the question—and it had profound theological and congregational implications.

For some in the Corinthian congregation there was no crisis, no conundrum, no dilemma, and Paul takes their side in verse 4. "We know," Paul writes, "that 'no idol in the world really exists,' and that 'there is no God but one.'" Armed with the theological assertion of monotheism—that one and only one God exists—Paul concludes that when, where, why, and by whom an animal is butchered is irrelevant for Christian faith and practice. In fact, in verse 10 Paul goes so far as to imply that it might be acceptable to eat that meat in the very temple of the god to whom it had been offered, because "there is no God but one." For Paul, the theological argument of monotheism was strong enough to alleviate the problem of religious pluralism altogether: There is no problem because there is no God but one.

But in verse 5, immediately after his assertion of monotheism as the solution to the problem, Paul steps back from his own theology, his own argument, his own ethic, to acknowledge that there is another perspective on the matter, a perspective in relation to which it is necessary to proceed with great care and humility. "Indeed," he writes in verse 5, "there may be so-called gods in heaven or on earth—as in fact there are many gods and many lords." Most Christian commentators on verse 5 are quick to say something like, "Paul doesn't really believe in these 'so-called gods,'" but that's not the point. The point is that Paul recognizes that for some people in the church at Corinth, the gods and lords of other faiths are a real concern, even if for him and for some others they are not. And so, just as in verse 4 he had taken the side of those who said "no problem" to eating meat that had been offered to idols, he turns in verse 9 to take the side of those for whom it was a real and present problem. On their behalf he writes, "Take care that this liberty of yours does not somehow become a stumbling block to the weak. For if others see you, who possess knowledge, eating in the temple of an idol, might they not, since their conscience is weak, be encouraged to the point of eating food sacrificed to idols?" and thereby "wound their conscience," he says in verse 12. Paul offers a global summary of this perspective in 10:23-24 where he writes, "'All things are lawful,' but not all things are beneficial. 'All things are lawful,' but not all things build up. Do not seek your own advantage, but that of the other."

Notice, please, that Paul did not attempt to solve this diversity challenge in the church at Corinth by saying, "All of you must think alike, believe alike, and behave alike." Instead, he said, "You must 'take care' with one another. You must 'build up' one another—however differently you may think, however differently you may believe, and however differently you may behave. "'Do not seek your own advantage, but that of the other.'" Notice also that Paul expertly modeled this counsel in chapter 8 by standing up for—by taking the side of—both those for whom eating meat that had been offered to idols created a crisis of conscience and those for whom it was no crisis whatsoever. Paul did not straddle the fence on the matter. He leaped into the field on one side of the fence and said to those standing on the other side, "Do you see these folk over here? Here is what they believe. Take care on account of them. Build them up." And then, he leaped over the fence into the field on the other side and said to those with whom he had just been standing, "Do you see these folk over here? Here is what they believe. Take care on account of them. Build them up." Just so, the apostle Paul modeled for us a mode of responding to diversity within our own communities that is not predicated on prevailing over one another but on building one another up, even those with whom we disagree. It is a mode of responding to diversity that is not grounded in overcoming or marginalizing one another, but on standing shoulder to shoulder with one another, even with those with whom we disagree or differ. We find unity in diversity, Paul says, not by seeking our own advantage but by seeking the advantage of one another, mutually and together.

To be sure, a diversity-in-unity kingdom requires changes in attitude, perception, and behavior from all of us. The wolves must stop growling and baring their teeth around the lambs, and the lambs must stop bleating at the sight of the wolves. The lions must stop stalking the calves, and the calves must stop quivering at the smell of the lions. The asp must not strike, and the nursing child must not strangle. A diversity-in-unity kingdom requires forbearance on the part of all of us, building up and seeking the advantage of one another rather than of ourselves.

In his inspiring and cantankerous little book *The Art of Humane Education*, Donald Phillip Verene makes an assertion about philosophy and education that is equally true of Christian faith. He writes:

> [A]rgument can never settle anything. Despite this defect of argument—that for every argument there is always a good counterargument—we should not become enemies of argument. In intellectual exchange argument can serve to bring out the features of a claim. But in our time argument . . . has become an intellectual fetish.[2]

Furthermore, says Verene, "Argument is always a partial way of thinking. . . . [A]rguments are never in themselves wisdom. . . . In the place of argument as the leading form of instruction I would put the question as the fundamental device."[3]

The question. We encounter the question as the leading form of instruction in the divine-human encounter from Genesis 3, "What is this that you have done?" (v. 13), to Mark 8, "Who do you say that I am?" (v. 29). We encounter the question as the fundamental device in the experience of faith from Psalm 22, "My God, my God, why have you forsaken me? Why are you so far from helping me, from the words of my groaning?" (v. 1) to Mark 4, "Who then is this, that even the wind and the sea obey him?" (v. 41). Faith, like philosophy and education (and love also, for that matter), is not an argument but always a question, a question with an uppercase Q, a question of existential and epistemological and ontological proportions, an intellectual and spiritual "feeling out of sight / For the ends of Being and ideal Grace."[4]

So I conclude not with an argument but with a question. Will you straddle the fence or will you leap it? Will you be content simply to argue with one another—some standing and some sitting, with those who are standing yelling at those who are sitting to stand up and those who are sitting yelling at those who are standing to sit down? Or will you covenant with God and with one another to work to understand one another, to "take care" with one another, stand up for one another—or to sit down for one another, as the case may be—and build one another up? Will you settle for anything less than the vision of the diversity-in-unity kingdom of God in which, "The wolf shall live with the lamb, the leopard shall lie down with the kid, the calf and the lion [shall feed] together. . . . They will not hurt or destroy on all my holy mountain; for the earth will be full of the knowledge of the LORD"? Will you?

CHAPTER 2

BIBLICAL RESPONSES TO DIVERSITY: CONQUEST, COEXISTENCE, AND COERCION

We were chatting pleasantly at a suburban children's play place when the talk turned suddenly not so small. "So you teach the Bible," he said in a tone of voice that made me wish I had told him I was a CPA, an engineer, or even a proctologist. "Well, here's what I want to know. When's the church going to start teaching the whole Bible instead of just part of it? I'm fed up with all this 'love-your-enemies' garbage. I've had all the 'turn-the-other-cheek' crap I can stand. When's the church going to start teaching the whole Bible and tell people the truth that to save this country we need to make like Joshua and drive all the unbelievers out of the land? That's what I want to know," he said. I stood in silence, momentarily stunned by what I had just heard. When I answered, it was softly; I was a bit dazed by the incongruity of this religious diatribe delivered at a four-year-old's birthday party. "Well," I said, "somehow

I've always thought that being a Christian was more about following Jesus than making like Joshua. I could be wrong, I guess, but that's what I've always thought."

Anyone observing our conversation from a distance would have seen no particular evidence of diversity in the encounter: two suburban American white males, about the same age, parents of children the same age, socioeconomic peers; confessing Christians, too. And yet, our perspectives on faithful Christian living in relation to people different from ourselves could hardly have been much more divergent. As I drove home that afternoon reflecting on my surprise encounter with this troubling attitude of a fellow Christian, I realized that whatever I might choose to say about his perspective, I could not say that it was "unbiblical." At the same time, however, I had a suspicion that "teaching the whole Bible instead of just part of it" would challenge my make-like-Joshua coreligionist with a much wider range of biblical responses to diversity than he was aware of. Along with examples of *conquest* or annihilation, the Old and New Testaments also clearly exhibit coexistence—living together—and coercion as responses to diversity.

CONQUEST

The *conquest response* to diversity is widely attested in the Bible. Its epitome is found in the story of ancient Israelite invaders at the gates of the far more ancient city of Jericho in the book of Joshua. Joshua 6 presents a highly stylized narrative echoing the "six days and a seventh" of creation in Genesis 1 (Joshua 6:3-4, 14-15). No mere military action, the battle of Jericho is the original biblical "worship war," complete with a liturgical procession of priests, the ark of the covenant, blowing shofars, and the ritual shout of the presence of the Lord (*tĕrû'â*, v. 20). Right worship by the Israelite "true believers" wins the war with the "infidel" Canaanite inhabitants of the city.

The first twelve chapters of the book of Joshua champion conquest as the solution to the diversity tension that arose between Israelite and Canaanite populations. In a nutshell, this solution is to "[devote] to destruction by the edge of the sword all in the city, both men and women, young and old, oxen, sheep, and donkeys" (Joshua 6:21). And not Jericho alone, according to Joshua 10:40: "So Joshua defeated the whole land, the hill country and the Negeb and the lowland and the slopes, and all their kings; he left no one remaining, but utterly destroyed all that breathed." For some Jews and Christians alike, Joshua's biblical "cleansing" of the land is idealized as a faithful triumph depicting the highest obedience to God and the greatest leadership of God's people. For others, however, this biblical narrative idealizes genocide (extermination of an entire ethnic or national group) and looks no more legitimate than the Nazi Holocaust of World War II or the more recent efforts at "ethnic cleansing" in the former Yugoslavia, Rwanda, and the Sudan.

The "rules of engagement" by which the Israelites operated in this conquest mode are attributed in the book of Deuteronomy to Moses, Joshua's mentor and the greatest of all the Old Testament prophets, according to Deuteronomy 34:10: "Never since has there arisen a prophet in Israel like Moses, whom the LORD knew face to face." In Deuteronomy 20:16-17, Moses is said to have instructed:

> But as for the towns of these people that the LORD your God is giving you as an inheritance, *you must not let anything that breathes remain alive. You shall annihilate them*—the Hittites and the Amorites, the Canaanites and the Perizzites, the Hivites and the Jebusites—just as the LORD your God has commanded. (emphasis added)

Annihilation represents a prophetically endorsed response to diversity in the Bible.

Joshua and Moses are not alone in this genocidal predisposition. The stories about the prophet Elijah include episodes of deadly religious and political conflict with King Ahab of the powerful Omride dynasty in the northern kingdom of Israel. At the close of the famous contest on Mount

Carmel between Elijah and four hundred fifty prophets of Baal, 1 Kings 18:40 recounts, "Elijah said to [the Israelites], 'Seize the prophets of Baal; do not let one of them escape.' Then they seized them; and Elijah brought them down to the Wadi Kishon, *and killed them there*" (emphasis added). In translation, there is no subject immediately before the final verb in the verse—"killed." But in Hebrew, a single word at the end of the sentence contains the subject, verb, and object: "*he* killed them." In the end, then, the great prophet Elijah, the partisan for true faith in Israel, is portrayed as settling the religious score by massacring his religious opponents.

Religiously motivated violence is a common feature of the prophetic imagination. Mentored by Elijah, the young prophet Elisha sent a disciple to anoint a general named Jehu as king of Israel with a deadly prophetic commission. Second Kings 9:6-8, 10 reports the charge from the prophet:

> Thus says the LORD the God of Israel: . . . You shall strike down the house of your master Ahab, so that I may avenge on Jezebel the blood of my servants the prophets, and the blood of all the servants of the LORD. For the whole house of Ahab shall perish; I will cut off from Ahab every male, bond or free, in Israel. . . . The dogs shall eat Jezebel in the territory of Jezreel, and no one shall bury her.

Second Kings goes on to narrate a bloodbath with which Jehu's reign began, as he annihilated not only the house of Ahab (2 Kings 9:21-24, 30-37; 10:1-11, 15-17) but also as many members of the house of King Ahaziah of Judah as he encountered along the way (9:27; 10:12-14). Jehu's religious *coup de grace* was his invitation to a "solemn assembly for Baal" in Samaria to which "all the worshipers of Baal came, so that there was no one left who did not come. They entered the temple of Baal, until the temple of Baal was filled from wall to wall" (10:21). Once the hall was packed, Jehu commanded his guards and officers, " 'Come in and kill them; let no one escape.' So they put them to the sword" (v. 25), and Jehu fulfilled his prophetic commission. From Joshua to Jehu, from Moses to Elijah and Elisha, one common biblical response to diversity endorsed by prophetic partisanship is the annihilation of the "other"—conquest.

The preeminent conquest passage in the New Testament occurs in the book of Revelation. Employing the highly symbolic, grotesque imagery characteristic of apocalyptic literature, Revelation 19 depicts Christ, "The Word of God," as the messianic warrior leading "the armies of heaven" against the enemies of God.

> He is clothed in a robe dipped in blood, and his name is called The Word of God. And the armies of heaven, wearing fine linen, white and pure, were following him on white horses. From his mouth comes a sharp sword with which to strike down the nations, and he will rule them with a rod of iron; he will tread the wine press of the fury of the wrath of God the Almighty. On his robe and on his thigh he has a name inscribed, "King of kings and Lord of lords."
>
> Then I saw an angel standing in the sun, and with a loud voice he called to all the birds that fly in midheaven, "Come, gather for the great supper of God, to eat the flesh of kings, the flesh of captains, the flesh of the mighty, the flesh of horses and their riders—flesh of all, both free and slave, both small and great.". . . And the rest were killed by the sword of the rider on the horse, the sword that came from his mouth; and all the birds were gorged with their flesh. (vv. 13-18, 21)

In this horrific vision, the "messianic banquet" is the feast of birds of carrion on the flesh of the slaughtered opponents of Christ—indeed slaughtered by Christ, according to verse 21. Clearly, then, Christian totalitarianism, oxymoronic and mis-guided though it may be, can draw deeply from the wells of biblical apocalyptic and prophetic literature.

The conquest response to diversity shows up among the disciples of Jesus in the Gospel of Luke. Luke 9:52 reports that some of the disciples "entered a village of the Samari-tans to make ready" for Jesus' arrival. But the Samaritans refused to receive Jesus because "his face was set toward Jerusalem" (v. 53), an orientation that was anathema to the Samaritans for whom the only authentic place to worship was on Mount Gerizim, above the ancient city of Shechem. Two of Jesus' followers are reported to have reacted with a prophetic call for retribution: "When his disciples James and John saw it, they said, 'Lord, do you want us to command fire to come down from heaven and consume them?'" (v. 54).[1] In response to this conquest mentality, Jesus "turned and rebuked them," according to verse 55. The word translated "rebuked," *epetimēsen* in the Greek text, is the same verb that was used earlier in the chapter when Jesus "*rebuked the unclean spirit*" that had possessed a child (v. 42). Rhetorically, then, the conquest response from Jesus' disciples is equated in Luke with the activity of an unclean spirit. Later manuscripts of the Gospel of Luke emphasize the point by expanding Jesus' words to his disciples in verse 55 to include, "He rebuked them, and said, '*You do not know what spirit you are of*, for the Son of Man has not come to destroy the lives of human beings but to save them'" (emphasis added). This textual addition to the words of Jesus is a savvy piece of inner-biblical interpretation in its emphasis on the nature of the "spirit" the disciples supposedly "are of"—in direct contrast to the "unclean spirit" of verse 42—if they are followers of Jesus. It rejects invoking the conquest model in the name of the one who came "not to destroy the lives of human beings but to save them.'" The Jesus of the Gospels evidently marches to the beat of a different drummer than the blood-drenched messianic warrior of the book of Revelation.

In the end, there are several weaknesses in the biblical conquest response to the frequently difficult, often dangerous, and sometimes deadly clash of diverse cultures and convictions. First, the gospel tradition presents conquest as a response that Jesus explicitly "rebukes" as exhibiting a spirit similar to the powers he came to overcome. Second, within the Old Testament itself, ancient Israel was never called on to recapitulate or repeat the conquest. Ritual reenactments of creation (the New Year's festival), the exodus from Egypt (Passover), the wilderness wandering (Feast of Booths), and the giving of the law (Pentecost) are well attested. But although God's gift of the land is frequently mentioned with expressions of gratitude and obligation alike, nowhere in the Bible is a "conquest day" or a "season of conquest" affirmed as a sacred ordinance, nor is conquest a mission to which Israel was ever called to fulfill yet again. Third, although proponents of annihilation are inclined to assert that conquest is a sign of obedience and trust in God, numerous biblical passages associate the conquest imperative with an underlying sense of insecurity or fear that in the encounter with other persons and perspectives, one's own faithfulness and fidelity will fail. Deuteronomy 20:17-18 is representative:

> You shall annihilate them—the Hittites and the Amorites, the Canaanites and the Perizzites, the Hivites and the Jebusites— just as the LORD your God has commanded, *so that they may not teach you to do all the abhorrent things that they do for their gods, and you thus sin against the LORD your God.* (emphasis added)

The rationale for conquest articulated here is religious insecurity, not faith: because your faith is not strong enough to resist temptation, you should exterminate the persons who are the source of the temptation. Finally, as the next section of this chapter will show, according to the Bible itself, the so-called "conquest" of the Canaanites simply did not happen the way Joshua 6 and 10:40 portray it.

COEXISTENCE

In contrast to the idealized, genocidal picture of a conquest portrayed in Joshua 1–12, the books of Joshua and Judges both attest that the Israelites *coexisted*—lived together—with the Canaanites in the land. Judges 1, for example, identifies significant populations of Canaanites who were not "utterly destroyed" as Joshua 10:40 claimed but who continued to inhabit the land along with the Israelites "after the death of Joshua" (1:1).

According to the book of Judges, the people of Judah "went and *settled with the Amalekites*" (Judges 1:16, emphasis added) instead of annihilating them. Judah "took possession of the hill country, but *could not drive out the inhabitants of the plain,* because they had chariots of iron" (v. 19, emphasis added). Similarly, "The Benjaminites *did not drive out the Jebusites who lived in Jerusalem; so the Jebusites have lived in Jerusalem among the Benjaminites* to this day" (v. 21, emphasis added). The list continues in verse 27, where

> Manasseh did not drive out the inhabitants of Beth-shean and its villages, or Taanach and its villages, or the inhabitants of Dor and its villages, or the inhabitants of Ibleam and its villages, or the inhabitants of Megiddo and its villages; but *the Canaanites continued to live in that land* (emphasis added).

The tribe of Ephraim "did not drive out the Canaanites who lived in Gezer; but *the Canaanites lived among them in Gezer*" (v. 29, emphasis added). As for Zebulun, they "did not drive out the inhabitants of Kitron, or the inhabitants of Nahalol; but *the Canaanites lived among them*" (v. 30, emphasis added). Asher and Naphtali were no more effective, as verses 31-33 report:

> Asher did not drive out the inhabitants of Acco, or the inhabitants of Sidon, or of Ahlab, or of Achzib, or of Helbah, or of Aphik, or of Rehob; but *the Asherites lived among the Canaanites,* the inhabitants of the land; for they did not drive them out.
> Naphtali did not drive out the inhabitants of Beth-shemesh, or the inhabitants of Beth-anath, but *lived among the Canaanites,* the inhabitants of the land. (emphasis added)

Finally, the unfortunate Danites could not even coexist with the Canaanites. According to verse 34, "The Amorites pressed the Danites back into the hill country; they did not allow them to come down to the plain."

Even the book of Joshua includes passages that indicate the coexistence of Canaanites and Israelites in the land of promise rather than the extermination of the indigenous population. Jerusalem was not taken, according to Joshua 15:63, nor was Gezer, according to 16:10. As in the book of Judges, Beth-shean, Ibleam, Dor, Taanach, Megiddo, and their surrounding villages continued to be populated by Canaanites (17:11-12). Although the "conquest narratives" of Joshua 1–12 have been seared into the popular religious imaginations of many Jews and Christians down through the centuries, the books of Joshua and Judges both attest that the Israelites did not annihilate the indigenous peoples in the majority of the most important population centers in Canaan. Instead, Israelites "lived among" Canaanites, and Canaanites "lived among Israelites." In other words, they *coexisted* in the land.

The book of Judges goes so far as to offer a variety of theological explanations for this condition of coexistence. One is that Israel's God left the indigenous peoples in the land as a punishment for the Israelites' failure to live by the covenant: "So the anger of the LORD was kindled against Israel; and he said, 'Because this people have transgressed my covenant that I commanded their ancestors, and have not obeyed my voice, I will no longer drive out before them any of the nations that Joshua left when he died'" (Judges 2:20-21). The two verses that follow present a second divine rationale—to "test" Israel's fidelity in the present and future rather than to "punish" infidelity in the past: "*In order to test Israel*, whether or not they would take care to walk in the way of the LORD as their ancestors did, the LORD had left those nations, not driving them out at once, and had not handed them over to Joshua" (vv. 22-23, emphasis added). A third rationale is offered in Judges 3:1-2 where the "test" is for a generation inexperienced with war: "Now these are the nations that the LORD left to test all those in Israel who had no experience of any war in Canaan (*it was only that successive generations of Israelites might know war,* to teach those who had no experience of it before)" (emphasis added). Regardless of the rationale one might prefer, the book of Judges asserts that the coexistence of Israelites and Canaanites in the land was divinely instigated and authorized.

According to Deuteronomy 32:8-9, that coexistence originates in creation: "When the Most High apportioned the nations, when he divided humankind, he fixed the boundaries of the peoples according to the number of the gods; the LORD's own portion was his people, Jacob his allotted share." According to this passage, the diversity of humankind—nations, peoples, and gods or religions—is part of the divinely created order. Rather than being a cause for conquest, social, political, and religious diversity *reflects the plan of God in creation.* The book of Genesis describes the diversity of the world's human population as the result of a peaceful expansion and diversification from "the descendants of Noah's sons" after the flood in Genesis 10: "These are the families of Noah's sons, according to their genealogies, in their nations; and from these the nations spread abroad on the earth after the flood" (v. 32). From the perspective of the larger narrative structure of Genesis 1–11, the proliferation and diversification of peoples throughout the earth is the result of the blessing of God originally given in creation (Genesis 1:28) and repeated to Noah and his offspring after the flood: "Be fruitful and multiply, and fill the earth" (Genesis 9:1). In the so-called "table of nations" in Genesis 10, all peoples are included within the envelope of the divine blessing "in their lands, with their own language, by their families, in their nations" (10:5, 20, 31), including the Canaanites in verses 15-19! Genesis 10 and Deuteronomy 32:8-9 affirm the quiet normalcy of a peaceable coexistence of peoples, nations, and religions in a world in which diversity is a divinely willed and blessed aspect of the created order.

The prophetic oracle in Jeremiah 27:2-6 reflects this vision of the apportionment of nations and lands in the prophet's present as well as in the primordial past:

> Thus the LORD said to me: Make yourself a yoke of straps and bars, and put them on your neck. Send word to the king of Edom, the king of Moab, the king of the Ammonites, the king of Tyre, and the king of Sidon by the hand of the envoys who have come to Jerusalem to King Zedekiah of Judah. Give them this charge for their masters: Thus says the LORD of hosts, the God of Israel: This is what you shall say to your masters: It is I who by my great power and my outstretched arm have made the earth, with the people and animals that are on the earth, and I give it to whomever I please. Now I have given all these lands into the hand of King Nebuchadnezzar of Babylon, my servant, and I have given him even the wild animals of the field to serve him.

Here Nebuchadnezzar, king of Babylon, is referred to as God's "servant" to whom the land has now been given. In this passage, being an "unbeliever" or nonbeliever does not disqualify one from being a "servant" of God, nor does it qualify one to be "driven from the land." Regardless of belief or its absence, a "servant" of God is depicted as one through whom God is accomplishing God's purpose in the world, whether "the people of God" are in tune with God's purpose or not.

This comprehensive perspective on the activity of God in the world is evident in Isaiah 45:1-4, a divine oracle that declares that it is the God of Israel who is behind the military successes of the founder of the Persian empire, Cyrus II, in spite of the fact that Cyrus does not even know the God who is causing him to prosper. The Persian empire-builder is even referred to as the Lord's "messiah," or anointed (v. 1):

> Thus says the LORD to his anointed, to Cyrus,
>   whose right hand I have grasped
> to subdue nations before him
>   and strip kings of their robes,
> to open doors before him—
>   and the gates shall not be closed:

I will go before you
  and level the mountains,
I will break in pieces the doors of bronze
  and cut through the bars of iron,
I will give you the treasures of darkness
  and riches hidden in secret places,
so that you may know that it is I, the LORD,
  the God of Israel, who call you by your name.
For the sake of my servant Jacob,
  and Israel my chosen,
I call you by your name,
  I surname you, though you do not know me.

As in Deuteronomy 32 and Jeremiah 27, God is understood to be actively and positively involved in the history of nations other than Israel and in the lives of "unbelievers"—or, more appropriately, believers in other deities.

One of the clearest and most compelling statements of coexistence is put forward in Jeremiah's so-called "letter to the exiles" in Jeremiah 29. After Nebuchadnezzar's successful military campaign against Jerusalem, which resulted in the deportation of King Jehoiachin, the royal court, and "the elite of the land," including elders, priests, prophets, artisans, and craftsmen (2 Kings 24:10-16; Jeremiah 29:1-2), Jeremiah is reported to have sent a letter to the community in exile containing a message that must have been received as equally comforting and chilling.

> Thus says the LORD of hosts, the God of Israel, to all the exiles whom I have sent into exile from Jerusalem to Babylon: Build houses and live in them; plant gardens and eat what they produce. Take wives and have sons and daughters; take wives for your sons, and give your daughters in marriage, that they may bear sons and daughters; multiply there, and do not decrease. But seek the welfare of the city where I have sent you into exile, and pray to the LORD on its behalf, for in its welfare you will find your welfare. (29:4-7)

Jeremiah counsels that the exiles should settle into their new Babylonian context and establish there the quiet normalcy of building homes and living in them, planting gardens and eating their produce, marrying and giving in marriage. They should go on about the business and pleasure of *multiplying there*, consistent with the divine blessing in creation (Genesis 1:28) and after the flood (Genesis 9:1). Furthermore, they are to *pray for their captors and the land of their captivity* because their own peace and well-being are inextricably tied to the peace and well-being of the pagan land in which they now live. Those who would pray for the peace of Jerusalem (Psalm 122:6) must also pray for the peace of Babylon!

In the New Testament, in the collection of sayings of Jesus known as the Sermon on the Mount, the coexistence response to diversity is emphasized in Matthew 5:43-45:

> You have heard that it was said, "You shall love your neighbor and hate your enemy." But I say to you, Love your enemies and pray for those who persecute you, so that you may be children of your Father in heaven; for he makes his sun rise on the evil and on the good, and sends rain on the righteous and on the unrighteous.

Reflected in this teaching of Jesus is a divinely created order featuring the coexistence of the diversities of "neighbors" and "enemies," "evil" and "good," "righteous" and "unrighteous," for all of whom God provides. Jesus' famous aphorism in response to the question posed to him about paying Roman imperial taxes fits well within this framework. The saying, "Give to the emperor the things that are the emperor's, and to God the things that are God's," in Mark 12:17 is more than a witty escape from the razor's edge of an inner-Jewish debate over the legitimacy of supporting the pagan regime and its cult by paying taxes. It is a reflection of a larger picture of the coexistence in the world of the kingdom of God with the kingdoms of earth, like the wheat and the weeds that "grow together until the harvest" (Matthew 13:30).

The apostle Paul writes out of this wider vision when he

counsels obedience to governmental authorities in Romans 13:1: "Let every person be subject to the governing authorities; for there is no authority except from God, and those authorities that exist have been instituted by God." This admonition is entirely consistent with the picture of the appointment of the nations in Deuteronomy 32:8-9 and the letter to the exiles in Jeremiah 29:4-8. At the same time, it is quite remarkable in Paul's first-century context, since it constitutes an affirmation of the legitimacy and divine sanction of the pagan Roman imperial authorities. Paul's and Jesus' counsel both imply that it is entirely possible—indeed, it is necessary—to be simultaneously a good citizen of a (pagan) temporal empire and a good citizen of the kingdom of God.

From Genesis to Jesus, from Joshua to Paul, coexistence—living together—is affirmed as a biblical response to diversity. Nevertheless, there is ample evidence that the proclaimers of coexistence have been highly unpopular in many circles. The prophet Hananiah in Jerusalem (28:1-11) and the prophet Shemaiah in Babylon (29:24-32) publicly opposed Jeremiah. The pro-Cyrus oracle in Isaiah 45 is followed immediately by a prophetic defense cast in the form of "woes" against those who take issue with the divine intention to work through a messiah who does not even know the Lord (vv. 9-13). Jesus' vision of the coexistence of good and evil, loving enemies, and praying for persecutors has fallen on deaf ears in every generation, including his own; and Paul's perspective that pagan governments are divinely ordained was lost already by the time of the writer of the book of Revelation, who chose to demonize the Roman authorities. Still, in the face of the call to "make like Joshua," there is an equally biblical response to diversity that says, "As for me and my house, we will follow Jesus and Paul" by espousing peaceable coexistence with others rather than annihilation of them.

COERCION

"Conquest" and "coexistence" are not the only responses to diversity evident in the Bible. It turns out that "teaching the whole Bible instead of just part of it" involves much more than the simple dichotomy between "making like Joshua," as my conversation partner put it, and "following Jesus," as I countered. *Coercion*, for example, is a response to diversity situated between conquest and coexistence: it is either a kinder, gentler conquest or a sinister variation on coexistence.

Coercion entails the subjugation or domination of one party by another, and it is featured prominently in the biblical portrayal of relations between Israelites and Canaanites. According to the books of Joshua and Judges, the relationship between the Canaanites and the Israelites in the land often involved the domination of one by the other. Joshua 17:12-13 presents a scenario of failed conquest followed by temporary coexistence and eventual coercion: "The Manassites could not take possession of those towns [failed conquest]; but the Canaanites continued to live in that land [peaceful coexistence]. But when the Israelites grew strong, they put the Canaanites to forced labor [coercion]." Subjecting the Canaanite inhabitants of the land to "forced labor" is a recurring refrain in Judges 1 (vv. 28, 30, 33, 35). The stories of the "judges" or tribal leaders that follow depict shifting conditions of coercion, as Israelites are reported to have been repeatedly subjugated by surrounding peoples (Cushan-rishathaim of Aram-naharaim in 3:8, Eglon of Moab in 3:14, Jabin of Canaan in 4:2-3, Midianites in 6:1-2, Philistines and Ammonites in 10:7-9, and Philistines again in 13:1). In the book of Judges, Israelite and Canaanite coexistence in the land appears to be characterized above all by their shifting capacities for domination of each other.

Late in the book of Judges, intra-Israelite coercion becomes the issue, as Israel's difficulties in the land are depicted not as a problem with other peoples but with one another. The narrator of Judges diagnoses the problem as a lack of authority at the top and a surplus of individual judgment throughout society: "In those days there was no king in Israel" (17:6; 18:1; 19:1; 21:25) with the result that "all the people did what was right in their own eyes" (17:6; 21:25). The implication is that a king would make things right by reducing individual decision making and eliminating the ensuing diversity of behavior. Israel's last "judge," Samuel, who depicts monarchy itself as coercive and oppressive, subsequently puts forward a dissenting opinion (1 Samuel 8:9-17). In contrast to the deliverance from oppression by enemies that always came in the book of Judges when the Israelites cried out to be saved, Samuel warns, "And in that day you will cry out because of your king, whom you have chosen for yourselves; but the LORD will not answer you in that day" (v. 18). Monarchy, it would appear, is an unpardonable sin.

After the death of Saul, Israel's first king, the divergent opinions about monarchy shift from promonarchical and antimonarchical sentiments to the choice between two competing dynastic houses. David, the son of Jesse, is acclaimed king in the southern city of Hebron (2 Samuel 2:4), while Ishbaal, the son of Saul, becomes king "over all Israel" in the Transjordanian town of Mahanaim (2:8-10). The rivalry between these two houses—"of David" and "of Saul," as they are called—subjected the land to yet another round of military conflict, according to 3:1: "There was a long war between the house of Saul and the house of David; David grew stronger and stronger, while the house of Saul became weaker and weaker." Peace through subjugation—beating the other into submission—is a storied biblical response to diversity, and it was the vehicle by which David united the kingdom under his rule.

Kingship and coercion are inseparable in the biblical narrative. The succession story—and the success story—of Solomon are associated with the assertion that "his kingdom was firmly established" (1 Kings 2:12). This statement forms a literary "inclusio," or "bookend," with the statement at the end of the chapter: "So the kingdom was established in the hand of Solomon" (2:46). In between these two references to the establishment of the kingdom are a series of incidents involving the elimination of individuals who would constitute either a direct threat to Solomon's authority or an indirect threat because they were old enemies of his father, David. Furthermore, to accomplish his ambitious building program (1 Kings 9:15-19), Solomon is said to have utilized the *corvee*—forced labor—of indigenous peoples, a practice seen previously in the books of Joshua and Judges:

> All the people who were left of the Amorites, the Hittites, the Perizzites, the Hivities, and the Jebusites, who were not of the people of Israel—their descendants who were still left in the land, whom the Israelites were unable to destroy completely—these Solomon conscripted for slave labor, and so they are to this day. (vv. 20-21)

Solomon's purported capacity to dominate others both inside and beyond the land is a key claim to his success as a regional monarch. According to 1 Kings 4:21: "Solomon was sovereign over all the kingdoms from the Euphrates to the land of the Philistines, even to the border of Egypt; they brought tribute and served Solomon all the days of his life."

The coercive and exploitive nature of Solomon's rule is brought to the fore after his death by representatives of the northern tribes who appeal to Solomon's successor, Rehoboam, for relief from the taxation and forced labor they experienced under Solomon. They say to the new king, "Your father made our yoke heavy. Now therefore lighten the hard service of your father and his heavy yoke that he placed on us, and we will serve you" (1 Kings 12:4). Rehoboam's older advisors, veterans of his father's administration, are reported to have recommended concessions as they attempted to turn the young monarch to a vision of kingship that would entail the king's serving the people as well as the people's serving the king: *"If you will be a servant to this people today* and serve them, and speak good words to them when you answer them, *then they will be your servants forever"* (v. 7, emphasis added).

However, "the young men who had grown up with him and now attended him" (v. 8) counseled Rehoboam—and a bit lewdly at that—"thus you should say to them, 'My little finger is thicker than my father's loins. Now, whereas my father laid on you a heavy yoke, I will add to your yoke. My father disciplined you with whips, but I will discipline you with scorpions'" (1 Kings 12:10-11). Following the counsel of his peers, Rehoboam turned a deaf ear to the northerners' appeal. "When all Israel saw that the king would not listen to them, the people answered the king, 'What share do we have in David? We have no inheritance in the son of Jesse. To your tents, O Israel! Look now to your own house, O David.' So Israel went away to their tents. . . . There was no one who followed the house of David, except the tribe of Judah alone" (12:16, 20b). The "united kingdom" was no more. Although the Davidic-Solomonic era is championed in some circles both biblical and postbiblical as a "golden era" of ancient Israelite history, the monarchy under David and Solomon is at the same time an excellent example of a failed attempt at unity by coercion.

Coercion is attested in the New Testament as an acceptable part of the social order, especially in relation to slaves and women. The institution of slavery is explicitly affirmed in admonitions such as, "Slaves, obey your earthly masters with fear and trembling" (Ephesians 6:5) and "in everything" (Colossians 3:22). Titus 2:9-10 transposes the submission of slaves from a typical Greco-Roman "house rule" into a theological principle by relating the slaves' behavior to "the doctrine of God": "Tell slaves to be submissive to their masters and to give satisfaction in every respect; they are . . . to show complete and perfect fidelity, so that in everything they may be an ornament to the doctrine of God our Savior." The exhortation that follows in verse 11 asserts that salvation has come to all, but salvation and emancipation are clearly separate issues for the author of the book of Titus.

In a frequently cited passage in Galatians 3:28, the apostle Paul asserts that in the community of the redeemed, the ethnic, economic, and social distinctions of the world do not apply: "There is no longer Jew or Greek, there is no longer slave or free, there is no longer male and female; for all of you are one in Christ Jesus." However, in his letter to the slave owner Philemon, Paul is so mincingly diplomatic that there is no consensus among modern commentators as to what Paul's precise intentions for the slave Onesimus are. He exhorts Philemon to treat Onesimus "no longer as a slave but more than a slave, a beloved brother" (v. 16), while at the same time sending Onesimus back to the master who owns him (v. 12). It is certainly the case that slavery in the Jewish and Greco-Roman world of the first century was a very different social and economic institution than the race-based chattel slavery of the American colonies and early states.[2] Nevertheless, it is no wonder that slavery could be supported so vociferously from the pulpits of many American churches in the eighteenth and nineteenth centuries given the explicit endorsement of it in the New Testament.

The teachings of Jesus include sayings and parables that employ the imagery of slavery without any comment on the fundamentally coercive and exploitive nature of the institution. For example, Jesus' parable in Luke 12:35-38 contains a status-reversing image of the master serving the slaves at the table (v. 37), but it leaves the assumptions of the status quo untouched when it affirms, "Blessed are those slaves" (vv. 37, 38). The illustration from everyday life in Luke 17:7-10 is a challenging corrective to a self-centered sense of entitlement among the followers of Jesus.

> Who among you would say to your slave who has just come in from plowing or tending sheep in the field, "Come here at once and take your place at the table"? Would you not rather say to him, "Prepare supper for me, put on your apron and serve me while I eat and drink; later you may eat and drink"? Do you thank the slave for doing what was commanded? So you also, when you have done all that you were ordered to do, say, "We are worthless slaves; we have done only what we ought to have done!"

The corrective is clear, but the uncritical acceptance of slavery as an acceptable part of the social order and the implicit exoneration of exploitive and insensitive treatment of other human beings are disconcerting—and especially so in the teachings of Jesus.

The important role of women in the ministry of Jesus (e.g., Mark 15:40-41; Luke 8:1-3) has been widely noted by commentators, as has Jesus' teachings that protected wives from divorce on trivial grounds (Matthew 19:3-9). However, the canonical teachings of Jesus say little or nothing that directly addresses the essentially coercive, male-dominated structures of Jewish and Greco-Roman society in the first century. When those structures are explicitly addressed in the New Testament, they tend to be affirmed—at least on the surface—as in Paul's counsel, "I want you to understand that Christ is the head of every man, and the husband is the head of his wife" in 1 Corinthians 11:3. The plain sense of this statement is inherently hierarchical. Only by taking the long way around—for instance, through an explication of the nature of Christ's self-emptying and humbling condescension (Philippians 2:7) as one who "came not to be served but to serve" (Mark 10:45)—can this statement be redeemed from its embeddedness in an essentially discriminatory and domineering social order.

Historical-critical interpreters of the Bible are fond of addressing this dilemma by excising—or at least "bracketing"—passages offensive to modern sensibilities as later historical developments in the practice of the earliest church. The best example of this perspective's making its way into the text itself is the decision of the translators and editors of the NRSV to place parentheses around 1 Corinthians 14:33b-36, which reads:

> As in all the churches of the saints, women should be silent in the churches. For they are not permitted to speak, but should be subordinate, as the law also says. If there is anything they desire to know, let them ask their husbands at home. For it is shameful for a woman to speak in church. Or

did the word of God originate with you? Or are you the only ones it has reached?

Setting these verses apart as more consistent with the perspective of the later "Pastoral Epistles," as in 1 Timothy 2:11-12 and Titus 2:5, than with Paul's approach (as exemplified in Galatians 3:28 but not in 1 Corinthians 11:3!) solves the dilemma of the diversity of Scripture on this point only if the authority of historical-critical scholarship has replaced the authority of the canon in the teaching of the church. "Teaching the whole Bible instead of just part of it" turns out to be an exercise that offends both liberals and conservatives in today's church.

Nowhere in the New Testament is coercion as a response to diversity more powerfully affirmed than in its apocalyptic passages. The so-called "letters to the seven churches" in the book of Revelation contain reflections of both internal and external diversity tensions, all of which are resolved in a moral exhortation capped by a recurring "victory formula" that begins, "To everyone who conquers," or a variation on it (Revelation 2:7, 11, 17, 26, 28; 3:5, 12, 21). Commentators generally agree that this "victory" refers to perseverance in the faith and the spiritual endurance of the small and sometimes persecuted Christian communities in Asia Minor rather than the literal annihilation of the opponents, a prerogative that belongs to the messianic warrior in chapter 19. Nevertheless, the conspiratorial inference of the repeated "anyone who has an ear listen to what the Spirit is saying to the churches" and the triumphalism of "conquering" is a potentially intoxicating rhetorical brew when read in a context of diversity tension.

At various points, the implication of the counsel to the seven churches looks dangerously coercive. To the church in Ephesus it is written:

> Yet this is to your credit: you hate the works of the Nicolaitans, which I also hate. Let anyone who has an ear listen to what the Spirit is saying to the churches. *To everyone who conquers, I*

will give permission to eat from the tree of life that is in the paradise of God. (2:6-7, emphasis added)

The identification of a group within the Christian community as persons whose works God "hates" and the assignment of divine "credit" for hating those whom God hates is divisive and disturbing counsel, especially in association with the ideal of overcoming or "conquering," spiritually or otherwise. The next message, to the church in Smyrna, introduces another element—the demonization of those who differ: Jewish adversaries are "a synagogue of Satan" (v. 9) and the Roman authorities are "the devil" (v. 10) with the power to imprison the faithful. The third exhortation, to the church at Pergamum, reiterates the demonization of external adversaries and then turns to the vilification of members of the Christian community, some of whom are disparagingly associated with the Mesopotamian seer Balaam of Numbers 22–24 fame. Without their repentance, divine "war against them" (v. 16) is sure to come. In the course of the first three "letters," the rhetoric of the exhortations has escalated from hatred through demonization and vilification to "holy war," an inflammatory model and a dangerous progression in responding to diversity.

At the close of a lengthy tirade to the church in Thyatira, the exhortation arrives at a decidedly temporal and political victory, whatever its spiritual intent:

I have this against you: you tolerate that woman Jezebel, who calls herself a prophet and is teaching and beguiling my servants to practice fornication and to eat food sacrificed to idols. . . . Beware, I am throwing her on a bed, and those who commit adultery with her I am throwing into great distress, unless they repent of her doings; and I will strike her children dead. . . . But to the rest of you in Thyatira, who do not hold this teaching . . . only hold fast to what you have until I come. *To everyone who conquers and continues to do my works to the end, I will give authority over the nations; to rule them with an iron rod*. (vv. 20-27, emphasis added)

From a "zero-tolerance" policy within the community of believers that vilifies internal opponents ("Jezebel," no less!), it is a small conceptual step to arrive at an iron-fisted rule "over the nations." In the message to the church in Philadelphia (3:7-13), those associated with the "synagogue of Satan" will be forced to "come and bow down before your feet" (3:9), a terrifyingly oppressive image for Jewish communities, especially in the afterglow of the power and authority promised in 2:26-27. The final "letter," to the church in Laodicea, closes with the famous image of Christ knocking at the door:

> Listen! I am standing at the door, knocking; if you hear my voice and open the door, I will come in to you and eat with you, and you with me. *To the one who conquers* I will give a place with me on my throne, *just as I myself conquered* and sat down with my Father on his throne. Let anyone who has an ear listen to what the Spirit is saying to the churches. (3:20-22, emphasis added)

An initially winsome and intimate religious image turns coercive and authoritarian in the end: the benefit of this table fellowship is access to the heavenly throne (v. 21). Behind the joy of having a place at the table lies the power-hungry ideal of exercising "authority over the nations; to rule them with an iron rod" (2:26-27).

There is an angle of vision according to which freedom and liberation are among the highest ideals of Christian Scripture. The deliverance of Israel from Egypt, Daniel from the lion's den, and Paul from incarceration in Philippi, among many other examples, all accord well with the paean in Psalm 146:7, "The LORD sets the prisoners free!" According to Luke 4:16-22, Jesus' inaugural sermon in the synagogue in Nazareth laid claim to the liberation mandate of Isaiah 61:1, "to bring good news to the oppressed, . . . to proclaim liberty to the captives, and release to the prisoners." And the Gospel of John declares, "If the Son makes you free, you will be free indeed" (John 8:36). This liberating ideal notwithstanding, coercion as a response to diversity is all too well attested in Scripture and in the church alike.

SO FAR AS IT DEPENDS ON YOU

A Sermon on Romans 12:9-21

In January of 1991, the Reverend Edmund Browning received a phone call. It was no ordinary call. It was the White House on the line. But then, Edmund Browning was no ordinary minister. He was at the time the Presiding Bishop of the Episcopal Church in the United States. President George H. W. Bush was calling to request the prayers and the support of the highest-ranking American clergyman in his communion as the preparations were being finalized for a military offensive to expel Iraqi armed forces from Kuwait. Browning promised his prayers, but he withheld his support. Instead, he advised his president and communicant that an invasion of Iraq would be inconsistent with the church's centuries-old criteria for determining a "just war" and that he would not support a war that was not consistent with the historic teaching of the church. Sometime later, the Reverend Billy Graham received a phone call. It was no ordinary call. It was the White House on the line. But then, the Reverend Billy Graham was no ordinary minister. Graham had been a friend and confidant of American presidents for decades, and once again he promised his president both his prayers and his support. In a nutshell, that's the story of how it happened that on the night of January 17, 1991, it was the Baptist evangelist Graham rather than the Episcopal bishop Browning who spent the night in the White House as Operation Desert Shield became Operation Desert Storm with the launch of air and missile strikes against Iraq.

This Browning-Graham dichotomy in the early 1990s is just one illustration of the challenge that faithful Christians the world over face as we attempt to discern an appropriate response to the wars and rumors of wars that rage around us and among us and between us, including the war on terrorism, the war in Afghanistan, the war in Iraq, culture wars, gender wars, mommy wars, age wars, and worship wars. The intermittent skirmishes, periodic battles, and sustained combat of the literal and figurative wars of our time confront us all with the challenge of discerning what our best Christian response as persons of faith and communities of faith might be in a highly polarized and deeply partisan time. Whereas simply quoting "what the Bible says" satisfies some people, it does not solve the larger dilemma. Graham and Browning are inveterate readers and veteran interpreters of Scripture, and they diverged in their assessments of the proper pastoral response to the request from their president and fellow Christian. Still, we turn to Scripture first for its counsel and for the counsel of the Holy Spirit at work in it and in us, and then we must go to work sorting out what our response will be, informed by Scripture and the Holy Spirit.

Turn with me to Romans 12:9-21. In Romans 12, the apostle Paul turns his attention from the great theological ideas he laid out in chapters 1–11 to address the shape of great and faithful living in the sunlight of those great ideas. Some people make the mistake of reading these words in Romans 12:9-21 as sweet-sounding spiritualisms. But the apostle Paul did not see the world through the rosy glow of stained-glass windows. I read Paul's words in Romans 12 as a first-century Christian version of what in German is called *Realpolitik*, a hard-nosed strategy for real living in the real world. In Romans 12:9-21, Paul was addressing a minority and marginal religious community living in a world that was rife with division, stricken with conflict, and saturated with violence. This small community of believers living in Rome had no control, no influence, and no evident way to affect the outcome of the chronic and acute conflicts that were flaring up throughout the Roman empire in which individuals and entire cultures struggled to adjust to changing political, social, economic, and religious landscapes while bearing the brunt of a double-barreled blast of Roman power and Hellenistic culture—in a word, a first-century "globalization."

Among Jews in Palestine, as among other peoples in other places in the empire, some reactions to the currents of change were violent and convoluted, wrapped in religious rhetoric and steeped in religious convictions. During the reign of the Hasmonean king and high priest Alexander Janneus, a six-year-long political and religious civil war is reported to have claimed more than fifty thousand Jewish lives. On one day alone, it is said, eight hundred Pharisees who opposed Janneus were crucified, their crosses lining the roads into Jerusalem. Paul, a Pharisee by training, according to his own account, would have been familiar with the slaughter of his predecessors in the faith. In addition, only a few years before Paul composed his letter to the church in Rome, thirty thousand Jews are said to have died in Jerusalem in an outbreak of violence that began as an altercation with Roman soldiers at the temple precinct during Passover. Paul was familiar with wars and rumors of wars, both literal and figurative, as cultures clashed and political, social, economic, and religious forces collided. By his own admission he was himself a perpetrator of such conflict and violence as a persecutor of "the Way" before he became his generation's greatest champion of it. Paul did not see the world in a rosy glow. He was no purveyor of sweet-sounding spiritualisms. Instead, he was a proponent of a powerful mode of being and believing for real living in the real world. What we receive from Paul in Romans 12 is remarkably savvy "diversity counsel" that clearly calls us to coexistence rather than to conquest or coercion.

In Romans 12:9-21, Paul reaches into the teachings of Jesus and the Old Testament wisdom tradition to offer one of the most pointed and compact summaries of Christian *Realpolitik* in the nearly two-thousand-year history of the church. The starting point for Paul's hard-nosed strategy for real living in the real world is an orientation that most of us quickly dismiss as sentimental and sappy, naive at best and self-defeating at worst, but which Paul put forward as a vital and tenacious way of being human. It begins with love, according to Paul: "Let love be genuine . . . love one another with mutual affection" (vv. 9-10). It is entirely counterintuitive to us—and probably to the Romans, as well—that Paul begins with love instead of with power. If Christian theology and practice in our time have missed the mark on one thing more than any other, it is our obsession with the exercise of power and our failure to practice love. The wielders of force in our world have seduced us, and we have sold our gospel birthright for a false sense of personal, national, and global security grounded in power.

When my middle son was ten years old, he inadvertently reminded me of the gospel alternative to our obsession with power. We were reading J. K. Rowling's *Harry Potter* books together as they were published. We were somewhere in the third book when we fell into a debate over who the most powerful wizard might be. He was holding out for Albus Dumbledore, the old graybeard who was headmaster at Hogwarts School where Harry and his friends were students. I, however, was championing young Harry himself. After all, Harry had survived the attack by the evil dark wizard Voldemort, and when Voldemort could not kill Harry, Voldemort's powers were temporarily broken. Hoping to cement my case for Harry's power, I asked, "Well, why do you suppose Voldemort couldn't kill Harry?" He was quiet for a moment, and I thought I had him stumped. But then he announced, "Because Harry's mother loved him so much and Harry loved her so much that Voldemort's evil could not defeat their love." The shingles fell from my eyes as I suddenly saw myself in the mirror of my young son's insight. In that mirror I saw a theologically trained parent in a spiritual straitjacket and analytical shackles fashioned by nineteenth- and twentieth-century intellectual giants from Nietzsche to Foucault, fixated on the analysis of power, while a ten-year-old proclaimed the gospel: it is not power but love that is the greatest deterrent to evil!

That's precisely the point that Paul makes by the structure of his discourse in verses 9-10 when he brackets evil inside a double admonition to love: "Let love be genuine; hate what is evil, hold fast to what is good; love one another with mutual affection." The very structure of Paul's sentence reveals that his response to evil is to surround it and counteract it with love, holding fast to what is good. The greatest danger you and I face right now in an age of partisanship and polemics, terrorism and warfare is not that we will fail to hate what we consider to be evil. No, the greatest danger is that in our zeal for hating evil, we will lose our hold on "what is good." In our zeal for winning the global conflict with Islamic extremists, there are those around us and among us who are stirring up hatred and prejudice against Islam and its adherents and against persons who have nothing in common with the perpetrators of terror other than their countries of origin or the faith they profess. In our zeal for responding effectively to "the terrorist threat" that the entire free world faces, there are those around us and among us who are eroding constitutional liberties and legal protections of the citizens of the very democracy that we are trying to defend against the terrorists. In our zeal to protect American national security, there are those around us and among us who are undoing centuries of military restraint, international cooperation, and the humane treatment of prisoners among the civilized nations of the world. We are all in grave danger of losing our hold on what is good in our zeal for hating what is evil because we are obsessed with power as the antidote to our world's ills.

But when Paul speaks of "zeal" in verse 11, he buries it in admonitions to show honor to others (v. 10), to "Serve the Lord. Rejoice in hope, be patient in suffering, persevere in prayer. Contribute to the needs of the saints; extend hospitality to strangers" (vv. 11-13). In a world of division, conflict, and violence, Paul calls the Christian community to be zealous for what is good, not zealous for retribution, conquest, or the exercise of power. Paul insists, "Do not repay anyone evil for evil, but take thought for what is noble in the sight of all" (v. 17). It is not enough, Paul says, to do what is noble in our own eyes; we must act on what is "noble in the sight of all." Unilateral vision is inadequate vision, according to Paul, because it takes into consideration only what we can see. Our vision of the noble is too often shortsighted and self-centered, and so the horizon of our vision must be expanded by attending to what is noble in the sight of others who see the world and us from an entirely different angle of vision than we do. When we see the world and ourselves through others' eyes, we arrive at a place of understanding and solidarity with all human beings, even understanding and solidarity with our enemies. And so Paul says, "Bless those who persecute you; bless and do not curse them" (v. 14). It is a savvy vision that Paul endorses, a vision that recognizes that at a fundamental level one's own well-being depends on the well-being of one's enemies. Paul stands in the tradition of the prophet Jeremiah, who called on the faithful in captivity in Babylon to "seek the welfare of the city where I have sent you into exile, and pray to the LORD on its behalf, for in its welfare you will find your welfare" (Jeremiah 29:7). Paul's *Realpolitik*, his diversity counsel, is grounded in the recognition that until those whom we count as our enemies are at peace, are made whole, and are made well, there will be no peace, wholeness, or wellness for us.

Praying for the peace of Babylon and blessing those who persecute you is the gospel tradition of Jesus of Nazareth, who announced in the Sermon on the Mount in Matthew's Gospel, "You have heard that it was said, 'You shall love your neighbor and hate your enemy.' But I say to you, Love your enemies and pray for those who persecute you, so that you may be children of your Father in heaven; for he makes his sun rise on the evil and on the good, and sends rain on the righteous and on the unrighteous" (Matthew 5:43-45). In the Gospel of Luke, Jesus' final assertion comes out slightly different: "You will be children of the Most High; for he is kind to the ungrateful and the wicked. Be merciful, just as your Father is merciful" (6:35-36). If God whom we worship and serve is "merciful" and "kind to the ungrateful and the wicked," how can we be any other way in the world and still be children of God? As servants of the God who "in all things . . . works for good" (Romans 8:28)[1] we are to "overcome evil with good," Paul says (Romans 12:21). He reaches into the ancient wisdom of Proverbs to say in Romans 12:20, "If your enemies are hungry, feed them; if they are thirsty, give them something to drink" (see Proverbs 25:21). After all, God has already treated us that well, Paul wrote in Romans 5:10, in that "while we were enemies" of God, still God provided for us when "we were reconciled to God through the death of his Son." Because we have received reconciliation instead of retribution, we are called to a ministry of reconciliation (2 Corinthians 5:18), not a ministry of retribution. Paul says, "Beloved, never avenge yourselves, but leave room for the wrath of God; for it is written, 'Vengeance is mine, I will repay, says the Lord' " (Romans 12:19; quoting Deuteronomy 32:35).

To be sure, it is not enough to merely quote Scripture. It is necessary for us to sort out how to live it also. In the late Thomas Merton's delightful little book *The Wisdom of the Desert*, an informal collection of stories and sayings of the so-called "desert fathers" of the fourth century, Merton passes along a story about a monk intent on revenge.

> One of the brethren had been insulted by another and he wanted to take revenge. He came to Abbot Sisois and told him what had taken place, saying: I am going to get even, Father. But the elder besought him to leave the affair in the hands of God. No, said the brother, I will not give up until I have made that fellow pay for what he said. Then the elder stood up and began to pray in these terms: O God, Thou art no longer necessary to us, since, as this brother says, we both can and will avenge ourselves. At this the brother promised to give up his idea of revenge.[2]

Whenever and wherever we decide to take affairs into our own hands to "repay anyone evil for evil," we are, in effect, living out an atheistic conviction that God is no longer necessary. We live in a time when it looks for all the world as though governments and nations, coalitions and alliances of nations are behaving as though God is no longer necessary as they settle international scores and enforce their individual or collective wills on one another.

But unlike the writer of the book of Revelation, Paul asserts in Romans 13 that even the pagan, imperial authority of Rome derives its authority "from God, and those authorities that exist have been instituted by God. . . . [T]he authority does not bear the sword in vain! It is the servant of God to execute wrath on the wrongdoer" (Romans 13:1, 4). According to Paul, there are times when the state must wield its sword as "the servant of God" to bring those who perpetrate evil in the world to justice. Fascinatingly, then, in Paul's *Realpolitik*, faithful service to God does not preclude service to the state—even an idolatrous and imperial state. Instead, Paul writes, "one must be subject" to the state,

> not only because of wrath but also because of conscience. For the same reason you also pay taxes, for the authorities are God's servants, busy with this very thing. Pay to all what is due them—taxes to whom taxes are due, revenue to whom revenue is due, respect to whom respect is due, honor to whom honor is due. (vv. 5-7)

Make no mistake about it: in Paul's diversity counsel, there is as at least as much room for conscientious service to the state—even service with a sword—as there is room for conscientious objection. Jesus is recorded in the Gospels as having been as merciful to a centurion as to any other sinner (Matthew 8:5-13), and the book of Acts does not equivocate in speaking of one who was "a devout man" (Acts 10:2) in the command of the centurion Cornelius. Jesus left the door wide open to such service when he advised, "Give to the emperor the things that are the emperor's, and to God the things that are God's" (Mark 12:17). Hear, then, the diversity challenge of Jesus and the apostle Paul alike to us in the church in times such as these: the militarists among us are called on to love and to pray for the pacifists among us, not to despise them; and the peacemakers among us are called to love and to pray for the warriors among us, not to revile them. And hear, then, the diversity challenge of Jesus and Paul for all of us together in our lives inside and outside the church: we are called on to love and to pray for those who are our opponents, adversaries, enemies even.

In a world of wars and rumors of wars, literal and figurative, Paul's counsel is this: "If it is possible, so far as it depends on you, live peaceably with all" (Romans 12:18). The imperative in Paul's counsel is "live peaceably with all." But notice the savvy of Paul, a man well acquainted with division, conflict, and violence. His exhortation to "live peaceably with all" is doubly qualified even before it is delivered: "if it is possible," he says, implying that it may not be; "so far as it depends on you," he says, implying that it may not. And so, you and I are left—not alone but together and with the counsel of the Holy Spirit at work in Scripture and in us—to ascertain the "if" and to discern the "so far," even as we commit ourselves to live peaceably with all by loving even our enemies and praying even for those who persecute us.

In the end, most of us are not likely to receive a phone call from the president requesting our prayers and our support. As the church in Rome was, we are a relatively small community of believers with no control, no influence, and no evident way to affect the outcome of the chronic and acute conflicts that are flaring up all around our world. But not one of us is exempt from the responsibility of attempting to discern an appropriate response, as individuals of faith in a community of faith, to the wars and rumors of wars that rage around us and among us and between us. And in times such as these, you and I can do no better than to take up the diversity counsel of Paul in a similarly trying era: Let love be genuine; hold fast to what is good; take thought for what is noble in the sight of all; and if it is possible, so far as it depends on you, live peaceably with all.

CHAPTER 3

BIBLICAL RESPONSES TO DIVERSITY: CONVERSION, COMPASSIONATE ACTION, AND CONVERSATION

In some circles of Christian faith and practice, the most frequently championed response to diversity is to transform differences—religious differences in particular—into similarities. The most common term for this transaction in which one party assimilates to another's religious norms or expectations is *conversion*. Another widely attested response is to look past differences to respond to human needs with *compassionate action* regardless of the attributes and attitudes of those in need. Also featured in the Bible and in Christian practice in at least some circles of the church is a high value on *conversation* that can lead to mutual understanding as well as enhanced self-understanding.

CONVERSION

A fourth biblical response to diversity is *conversion*. One option for addressing certain aspects of diversity is to convert key differences into similarities. Mark 16:15-16 asserts the underlying framework of this approach clearly and succinctly.

> Go into all the world and proclaim the good news to the whole creation. The one who believes and is baptized will be saved; but the one who does not believe will be condemned.

In this way of thinking, the world is divided neatly into the saved and the damned, and conversion is the balance on which the scales of divine judgment tip. Difference damns while similarity saves. Strictly speaking, the popular idea of a "religious conversion" develops much later than the Old and New Testaments. However, when an "outsider" becomes an "insider" by trading the faith or practice of one community for another, this transformation of a distinguishing difference into a distinctive similarity is at the heart of what will later be called "conversion."

A conversion response to diversity is exhibited in the Old Testament in a series of oracles in Isaiah 19:19-25 that anticipate the conversion of the Egyptians and the Assyrians to the worship of Israel's God:

> On that day there will be an altar to the LORD in the center of the land of Egypt, and a pillar to the LORD at its border. It will be a sign and a witness to the LORD of hosts in the land of Egypt; when they cry to the LORD because of oppressors, he will send them a savior, and will defend and deliver them. The LORD will make himself known to the Egyptians; and the Egyptians will know the LORD on that day, and will worship with sacrifice and burnt offering, and they will make vows to the LORD and perform them. . . . On that day there will be a highway from Egypt to Assyria, and the Assyrian will come into Egypt, and the Egyptian into Assyria, and the Egyptians will worship with the Assyrians.

On that day Israel will be the third with Egypt and Assyria, a blessing in the midst of the earth, whom the LORD of hosts has blessed, saying, "Blessed be Egypt my people, and Assyria the work of my hands, and Israel my heritage."

This blessing of Israel's God on Egypt and Assyria accompanies the Egyptians' and the Assyrians' coming to "know the LORD" and adopting Israelite modes of worship. Religious differences will disappear, replaced by similarities in faith and practice. The beatific vision of Isaiah 2:2-4 is better known and less cultic in its focus.

> In days to come
> the mountain of the LORD 's house
> shall be established as the highest of the mountains,
> and shall be raised above the hills;
> all the nations shall stream to it.
> Many peoples shall come and say,
> "Come, let us go up to the mountain of the LORD,
> to the house of the God of Jacob;
> that he may teach us his ways
> and that we may walk in his paths."

In the Old Testament, conversion is typically a visionary component of an ideal and eschatological future rather than an element of the present mission and identity of Israel.

Still, the book of Joshua recounts a conversion story in which an outsider became an insider to Israelite faith and practice. Rahab, the prostitute in Jericho who harbored the Israelite men sent to spy out the land and the city in Joshua 2, delivers one of the most stirring short confessions of faith in Israel's God in the entire account of ancient Israel's history in the land from Joshua to 2 Kings. She says to the men:

> I know that the LORD has given you the land, and that dread of you has fallen on us, and that all the inhabitants of the land melt in fear before you. For we have heard how the LORD dried up the water of the Red Sea before you when you came out of Egypt, and what you did to the two kings of the Amor-

ites that were beyond the Jordan, to Sihon and Og, whom you utterly destroyed. As soon as we heard it, our hearts melted, and there was no courage left in any of us because of you. The LORD your God is indeed God in heaven above and on earth below. (Joshua 2:8-11)

In return for aiding and abetting the conquest of Jericho, she exacts from the spies an oath sworn in the name of their God whom she has confessed as "indeed God in heaven above and on earth below" to save her and her family when they return to conquer the city. Four chapters later, after Jericho is taken, Joshua orders "the two men who had spied out the land, 'Go into the prostitute's house, and bring the woman out of it and all who belong to her'" (Joshua 6:22). Thus, "Rahab the prostitute, with her family and all who belonged to her, Joshua spared. Her family has lived in Israel ever since. For she hid the messengers whom Joshua sent to spy out Jericho" (v. 25)—and she confessed faith in Israel's God in good deuteronomistic fashion.

Another outsider who becomes an insider by committing herself to similarity over difference is the Moabite woman Ruth, the daughter-in-law of Naomi. When Naomi's husband and two sons, one of whom is Ruth's husband, die in Moab where Naomi's family had fled to escape a famine in Israel (Ruth 1:5), Ruth pledges herself to her mother-in-law with the memorable poetic lines:

> Do not press me to leave you
> or to turn back from following you!
> Where you go, I will go;
> Where you lodge, I will lodge;
> your people shall be my people,
> and your God my God. (Ruth 1:16-17)

Ruth has clearly committed to cross "the boundaries of the peoples according to the number of the gods" established in creation "when the Most High apportioned the nations, when he divided humankind," according to Deuteronomy 32:8.

Conversion—transforming certain differences into similarities—is not a one-way street, of course. As we have already seen in chapter 2 above, an underlying fear of the proponents of the conquest response to diversity in the Old Testament is that when they come into contact with Canaanites, Israelites might become worshipers of the Canaanites' deities. The first of Joshua's two "farewell addresses" at the end of the book of Joshua articulates that concern in an admonition to the Israelites:

> Therefore be very steadfast to observe and do all that is written in the book of the law of Moses, turning aside from it neither to the right nor to the left, so that you may not be mixed with these nations left here among you, or make mention of the names of their gods, or swear by them, or serve them, or bow yourselves down to them, but hold fast to the LORD your God, as you have done to this day. . . . Be very careful, therefore, to love the LORD your God. For if you turn back, and join the survivors of these nations left here among you, and intermarry with them, so that you marry their women and they yours, know assuredly that the LORD your God will not continue to drive out these nations before you; but they shall be a snare and a trap for you, a scourge on your sides, and thorns in your eyes, until you perish from this good land that the LORD your God has given you. (Joshua 23:6-8,11-13)

Although it is acceptable for a Canaanite such as Rahab and a Moabite such as Ruth to take up the worship of Israel's God, it is deemed unacceptable—but always an open possibility—for an Israelite to take up the worship of another deity.

In the New Testament, the paradigmatic conversion story is the experience of Saul of Tarsus on the road to Damascus. Recounted three times in the book of Acts (9:3-8; 22:6-21; 26:12-18), this story relates how it happened that a persecutor of "the Way" (9:2) reversed his mission to become his generation's greatest proponent of it. The shift in Saul's religious attitude and action is presented as radical enough that his allies have now become his enemies (9:23-24, 29), and his former adversaries are now his friends (9:25, 30). Still, as stories of "religious conversion" go, Saul's exhibits several peculiarities that would appear to be significant shortcomings for an epitome of the genre. Even after Saul (his name abruptly changes from the Jewish "Saul" to the more Hellenistic "Paul" in Acts 13:13) is set apart by the church in Antioch and sent out to proclaim the Way instead of persecute it (13:1-4), the book of Acts makes it clear that Paul continues to worship in the synagogue (13:14), continues to preach from the Jewish Scriptures ("the law and the prophets" in 13:15), continues to worship the God of *our* ancestors" (13:17, emphasis added), and continues to embrace the salvation-history of Israel (13:17-22). In other words, the religious *continuities* after Paul's so-called conversion far outnumber the discontinuities!

As radical as Paul's reorientation may be, he clearly does not "convert" from one religion to another in the later sense of conversion. When Paul visits Jerusalem, he goes to the temple to worship (Acts 21:26), hardly the action of someone who has "converted" from the Judaism of his upbringing. The deity he worships, the places where he worships, and the Scriptures he uses remain the same, as does his self-proclaimed identity as a Jew (Acts 22:3; 2 Corinthians 11:22; Galatians 2:15). In his own words, Paul received "a revelation" (Galatians 1:12, 16) and a "calling" for which he was "set apart" before he was born (1:15). Only by looking at Paul through the later lens of the eventual separation and evolution of "Christianity" from its birth mother, early "Judaism," can Paul's experience be misrepresented as a conversion from one religion to another. Instead of a "religious conversion," Paul experienced a "diversity conversion": in the aftermath of his Damascus road revelation, he comes to accept persons and champion a perspective that he had previously persecuted and despised.

Simon Peter's rooftop vision in Joppa (Acts 10:9-16) and his subsequent encounter with Gentiles and the Holy Spirit in Cornelius's house in Caesarea (10:24-48) together constitute another New Testament example of a diversity conversion. In his noonday vision, Peter sees

> the heaven opened and something like a large sheet coming down, being lowered to the ground by its four corners. In it were all kinds of four-footed creatures and reptiles and birds of the air. Then he heard a voice saying, "Get up, Peter; kill and eat." But Peter said, "By no means, Lord; for I have never eaten anything that is profane or unclean." The voice said to him again, a second time, "What God has made clean, you must not call profane." (Acts 10:11-15)

A curious aspect of this dream is that it implies that during his years in the inner circle of Jesus, it never occurred to Simon Peter to violate the boundaries of the Jewish dietary restrictions, an important marker distinguishing "insiders" from "outsiders" in faithful Jewish practice. The voice from heaven gives Peter a new set of instructions for dealing with diversity that the voice of the earthly Jesus evidently had not.

The boundary-erasing implication of Peter's vision is confirmed the next day in Caesarea when he discovers that God is at work in the lives of people whom Peter would previously have excluded from his fellowship. In the house of the centurion Cornelius, Peter acknowledges both his prior prejudice and his newfound perspective: "You yourselves know that it is unlawful for a Jew to associate with or to visit a Gentile; but God has shown me that I should not call anyone profane or unclean" (Acts 10:28). Peter's attitude shifts from a particularly conservative, isolationist perspective to an acceptance of persons he previously excluded as outsiders: "I truly understand that God shows no partiality, but in every nation anyone who fears him and does what is right is acceptable to him" (vv. 34-35). Not everyone in the church was pleased with Peter's new diversity maturity, as the next chapter of the book of Acts recounts: "When Peter went up to Jerusalem, the circumcised believers criticized him, saying, 'Why did you go to uncircumcised men and eat with them?' Then Peter began to explain it to them, step by step," recounting his vision in Joppa and his experience in Caesarea, at the end of which he concludes not with an argument but with a question—à la Verene—to his audience, "Who was I that I could hinder God?" (11:4-17). The narrator reports, "When they heard this, [his critics] were silenced" (v. 18).

As we have seen, chapters 9–10 of the book of Acts contain back-to-back diversity-conversion stories of central characters in the spread of the gospel and the growth of the early church: Paul and Peter both have conversion experiences that lead them to understand diversity boundaries that they once considered inviolable to divide no more. Both discovered that persons they thought to be anathema are accepted by God within the circle of God's blessing and activity in the world. In other words, their understandings of others, of God, and of themselves were transformed or converted.

COMPASSIONATE ACTION

Not every character in the Bible must be "converted" to deal kindly with persons different from themselves. *Compassionate action* is a response to diversity that looks beyond differences to respond to human commonalities, especially commonalities in human need. In the book of Deuteronomy, acting compassionately toward the poor and needy is not optional behavior but is required.

> If there is among you anyone in need, a member of your community in any of your towns within the land that the LORD your God is giving you, do not be hard-hearted or tight-fisted toward your needy neighbor. . . . Since there will never cease to be some in need on the earth, I therefore command you, "Open your hand to the poor and needy neighbor in your land." (Deuteronomy 15:7, 11)

In addition to economic need, social and legal standing that put persons at a disadvantage was to be addressed without discrimination, consistent with the nature and action of God, according to Deuteronomy 10:17-19.

> For the LORD your God is God of gods and Lord of lords, the great God, mighty and awesome, who is not partial and takes no bribe, who executes justice for the orphan and the widow, and who loves the strangers, providing them food and clothing. You shall also love the stranger, for you were strangers in the land of Egypt.

The rationale for compassionate action without regard for differences is clear: *God* looks past the differences to respond justly and mercifully to all persons.

In 2 Kings 5:2-4, an unnamed "girl from the land of Israel" epitomizes compassionate action when she looks past the impediments of national, religious, and societal differences to suggest that Naaman, the Syrian general in whose household she is a domestic slave, would be cured of his disease if he could pay a visit to "the prophet who is in Samaria" (v. 3). Why it occurred to this little girl to be compassionate enough to wish that her captor could be cured of an incapacitating malady is unclear. Perhaps she was a child who had been reared on proverbial wisdom, as in Proverbs 25:21—"If your enemies are hungry, give them bread to eat; and if they are thirsty, give them water to drink"—and she extrapolated from the power of food and water to sustain life to the power of prophetic healing to restore life. Or perhaps she recalled the salvation-history words of the Torah— or words like them—that she had been taught, "You shall love the alien as yourself, for you were aliens in the land of Egypt: I am the Lord your God" (Leviticus 19:34), and she innocently extended their interpretation to mean loving the alien in whose midst you are as well. It is impossible to get behind the text to reconstruct her experience and her attitude, but in the three verses in which she appears she is a model of compassionate action that looks right past the differences of nationality, religion, and coercive power structures to the commonality of human need. In particular, she exhibits a model of compassion that does not discriminate against the wealthy and the powerful any more than it does against the poor and powerless.

The unnamed girl is not the only remarkably compassionate character in this story. Elisha offers the healing counsel in verse 10: "Go, wash in the Jordan seven times" (although he does not so much as give Naaman the time of day by meeting with him in person, according to verse 11). But after Naaman has been healed and has confessed, "Now I know that there is no God in all the earth except in Israel" (v. 15), Elisha meets with the Syrian general in person and consents to an even more remarkable request than the healing: Naaman asks for a prophetic "pardon" so that he may continue to worship in the temple of "Rimmon," "thunderer," an epithet for the storm god Hadad—or Baal, as the storm god is more widely known in Canaanite circles. Naaman informs Elisha that in carrying out his official duties in Syria it will be necessary for him to accompany his master the king into the temple for worship. The incongruity of Naaman's new confession of faith with his impending practice in a temple of Baal is indicated by the fact that his "bowing down" in the Syrian temple is stated twice (as is his request for pardon): "When . . . I bow down in the house of Rimmon, when I do bow down in the house of Rimmon, may the LORD pardon your servant on this one count" (v. 18). Elisha's response, "Go in peace," authorizes Naaman's pluralistic practice—worshiping the Lord, the God of Israel while attending worship in a Syrian temple. This amazing allowance on the part of the prophet takes into consideration the considerable diversity tension of the religious, political, and social realities that a Syrian worshiper of an Israelite God will face.

In the New Testament, the epitome of compassionate action is found in Jesus' parable in Luke 10:30-35 about a Samaritan, a member of a religious minority traveling far from home, who "was moved with pity" (v. 33) and stopped to provide assistance to another traveler who had fallen "into the hands of robbers, who stripped him, beat him, and went away, leaving him half dead" (v. 30). Jesus' choice of a Samaritan as the protagonist of the parable and as the model in a discussion about "neighborliness" (v. 36) and what it takes "to inherit eternal life" is a lesson in diversity leadership. A religious "outsider" in the eyes of Jesus' audience is presented as exhibiting the attitude and behavior that "insiders" should emulate: "Go and do likewise," says Jesus (v. 37). Jesus' Jewish listeners would undoubtedly have been much more comfortable if he had said, "Make like Joshua," than they were when he said, "Make like a Samaritan."

In another parable in which things ultimate and eternal are at stake, Jesus commends compassionate action as the basis for the judgment of "all the nations" (NRSV)—or "all the Gentiles," as the Greek word *ethnē* is more frequently translated in the New Testament. In the judgment to come, according to the parable in Matthew 25:31-46, "the Son of Man" will separate the sheep (those who "inherit the kingdom") from the goats (who must depart "into the eternal fire") on the basis of their having met the needs of the hungry and thirsty, their welcoming the stranger, their clothing the naked, their care for the sick, and their visiting the imprisoned. In the current American setting in which this passage has become a biblical lynchpin in the proclamation of the social gospel and the propagation of Christian social action, the scandal of this parable in its original Jewish context is lost entirely. Jesus offers up yet another challenging lesson in religious diversity to his audience when his parable asserts that Gentiles—*pagans* in the eyes of his listeners—*will be saved*. The compassionate action of "outsiders" makes them "insiders" in the eyes of God and in the last judgment. If there is a "go-and-do-likewise" implication in this parable, it is found in the scandalous exhortation to "make like pagans" who act compassionately.

CONVERSATION

"How is it that you, a Jew, ask a drink of me, a woman of Samaria?" (John 4:9). This leading question expresses the surprise of an unnamed Samaritan woman to whom Jesus speaks at Jacob's well, and it identifies at the outset a set of diversity issues that have long been highlighted by commentators. Both the gender difference and the historic religious animosity between Samaritans and Jews should have been sufficient to keep these two people from interacting amicably together. The question also captures the disarming character of *conversation* between persons who might otherwise have nothing to do with each other. By the end of the encounter, the woman is so enamored of her conversation partner that she leaves her jar at the well to hurry into the nearby Samaritan city of Sychar to tell others to come out to meet and talk with this Jew. For his part, Jesus is so pleased with the exchange that he agrees to extend his stay among the Samaritans before continuing his journey to Galilee (vv. 40, 43). It is no ordinary conversation, of course, as the dialogue is peppered with prophetic, messianic, and eschatological elements. Nevertheless, it exemplifies the encounter on common ground—a community well—of two persons who are in some sense mutually "at each other's mercy" and who respond to that condition with grace and consideration for each other. Jesus is tired and thirsty, and the woman has a jar with which to draw water (vv. 6-7). She, however, thirsts for something more, something that he says he can offer her (vv. 13-15). A diversity encounter that could very well have been antagonistic and insulting on both sides turns out to be of mutual benefit thanks to the willingness and ability of the two parties to engage in open and honest conversation about their perceptions of each other and of themselves.

On another occasion, Jesus is far less sanguine. He is, in fact, antagonistic and insulting until the course of conversation changes his attitude and his action. Matthew 15 reports Jesus' encounter with another unnamed woman who is variously identified in the Gospels as a "Gentile," a "Syrophoenician," and a "Canaanite," in other words, a person who on account of gender, ethnicity, and religion an itinerant rabbi was likely to have nothing to do with. That was obviously Jesus' initial intention, according to Matthew's version of this incident. Unresponsive to her cries for "mercy" because of the torment her daughter was experiencing, Jesus ignored her appeal: "He did not answer her at all" (15:23). But she kept shouting after him, much to the annoyance of Jesus' followers, so he responded by clarifying for her the fact that his mission of teaching and healing was not intended for people such as her: "I was sent only to the lost sheep of the house of Israel" (vv. 23-24); in other words, not to Gentiles, Syrophoenicians, or Canaanites. But driven by her daughter's suffering, she responded to his rebuff with the explicit plea, "Lord, help me" (v. 25). Jesus, however, remained as insistent in his refusal as she was insistent in her appeal that she and her daughter be included in the circle of his mercy. This time, his response was insulting, as it employs a common early Jewish slur for Gentiles and prostitutes: "It is not fair to take the children's food and throw it to the *dogs*" (v. 26, emphasis added). It is a shameful statement, but apparently she was accustomed to this kind of insulting treatment from good religious people. Or perhaps her desperation over her daughter's condition made her immune to its sting, because she succeeded in delivering one of the greatest comeback lines in all of Scripture: "Yes, Lord, yet even the dogs eat the crumbs that fall from their masters' table" (v. 27). After ignoring, rebuffing, and insulting this woman, Jesus of Nazareth finally recognized in her a worthy conversation partner who had succeeded in overcoming his prejudice against her: "Woman, great is your faith! Let it be done for you as you wish" (v. 28).

Another example of a conversation that leads to a change of mind and action occurs between the beautiful and diplomatic Abigail and the rash young brigand David in 1 Samuel 25. The request by David's men to Abigail's wealthy and churlish husband Nabal for material provisions on account of their protection of Nabal's shepherds "in the wilderness" is rejected with an insult (vv. 5-11). When David hears of Nabal's response, he reacts by taking offense and marshalling an armed sortie to avenge the insult on Nabal and on his entire household (vv. 12-13, 21-22). When Abigail is informed of the looming crisis, she sets out to intervene (vv. 14-20). The reader has already been informed that Nabal is "so ill-natured that no one can speak to him" (v. 17). The only question that remains before Nabal's household is decimated and David, in turn, incurs bloodguilt for his reaction that far exceeds any reasonable response to the offense (v. 33) is whether or not David is a person who is capable of conversation. When Abigail encounters David, she begins by expressing her personal responsibility for what has happened (vv. 24-25), even as she acknowledges that it was the folly of Nabal (whose name means "fool" in Hebrew) that has elicited David's reaction. She presents David with the provisions that she has brought for his men and calls on him to forgive Nabal (vv. 27-28). She then goes on to point out that it is not Nabal alone who is in the wrong in this inflammatory turn of events. If David will listen to her, he will have "no cause of grief, or pangs of conscience, for having shed blood without cause" (v. 31). David's positive response to Abigail's intervention is as quick as his negative reaction to Nabal's offense: "Blessed be the LORD, the God of Israel, who sent you to meet me today! Blessed be your good sense, and blessed be you, who have kept me today from bloodguilt and from avenging myself by my own hand! . . . Go up to your house in peace; see, I have heeded your voice, and I have granted your petition" (vv. 32-33, 35). Unlike Nabal, with whom "no one can speak," David is capable of conversation—even conversation in the course of which his own folly is revealed to him. Rather than diversity of attributes (gender, ethnicity, religious affiliation), as in the previous example, this encounter features a conflict arising from attitudinal, perceptual, and behavioral diversity that is successfully negotiated through a conversation that reveals one's own shortcomings alongside the shortcomings one perceives in others.

Consistent with the behavior modeled by Abigail, the Sermon on the Mount in the Gospel of Matthew commends *conversation* between those who are at odds with each other. Jesus instructs his audience, "So when you are offering your gift at the altar, if you remember that your brother or sister has something against you, leave your gift there before the altar and go; first be reconciled to your brother or sister, and then come and offer your gift" (5:23-24). As a response to diversity of perception, attitude, or behavior, this admonition frames the matter as a concern for the reconciliation of persons rather than the resolution of a difference or an issue. What Jesus does not say is "settle the matter" or "come to agreement" or "see things eye-to-eye." Instead, he commends engaging in the kind of face-to-face conversation that reconciles persons regardless of the differences between them. Conversation rather than litigation is recommended in verse 25: "Come to terms quickly with your accuser while you are on the way to court with him." Later in Matthew's Gospel, the pithy council of the Sermon on the Mount is expanded into a casuistic procedure that insists on conversation at each step. It begins with private conversation between the person who feels wronged and the person by whom he or she feels wronged: "If another member of the church sins against you, go and point out the fault when the two of you are alone. If the member listens to you, you have regained that one" (18:15). If the initial conversation does not arrive at reconciliation, a second level of conversation is recommended: "But if you are not listened to, take one or two others along with you, so that every word may be confirmed by the evidence of two or three witnesses" (v. 16). If this expansion of the circle of the conversation does not arrive at a resolution, then the conversation is expanded yet again to include the congregation (v. 17). Following this process assures that differences in perception, attitude, and behavior— and along with them any accusations, insinuations, or innuendos—are to be aired in *direct conversation* among the principal parties involved, speaking *with each other instead of about each other* concerning whatever differences that exist.

In the biblical tradition, conversation is not limited to

human interaction but is characteristic of divine-human encounters as well. The rabbinic tradition has long held that the divine inquiry put to the man and the woman in the Garden of Eden, "Where are you?" (Genesis 3:9), was not intended to gather information but to elicit conversation. Rashi wrote that God "knew where he was but [He asked where Adam was] *to enter into conversation with him.*"[1] Similarly, Rashi commented in the case of Balaam in Numbers 22:9, God asks, " 'What men are these with thee?' to enter into conversation with them."[2] The paramount symbol of divine-human conversation in the Old Testament is the tent of meeting where "the LORD used to speak to Moses face to face, as one speaks to a friend" (Exodus 33:11). This conversational image is later applied to the entire congregation at Mount Sinai/Mount Horeb in Deuteronomy 5:4 where Moses characterizes the congregation's experience at the mountain as when "The LORD spoke with you face to face at the mountain, out of the fire."

When it comes to differences of attitude, perception, and behavior, the divine-human conversation *par excellence* in the Old Testament occurs on Mount Sinai in Exodus 32. While Moses lingered on the mountain, his whereabouts unknown to the people waiting below (32:1), the Israelites prevailed on Aaron to produce an image of the deity for them. The next day, when they observe a "festival to the LORD" utilizing Aaron's calf as the symbol of their God (v. 5), the divine reaction at the top of the mountain is quick and angry:

> The LORD said to Moses, "Go down at once! Your people, whom you brought up out of the land of Egypt, have acted perversely; they have been quick to turn aside from the way that I commanded them. . . . I have seen this people, how stiff-necked they are. Now let me alone, so that my wrath may burn hot against them and I may consume them."
> (Exodus 32:7-10)

Moses, apparently accustomed to such "in-your-face" conversation with God, responds brilliantly with a repartee worthy of a prophet, priest, or defense attorney. His opening salvo is a question that reminds God that the unruly crowd at the foot of the mountain is *"your* people, whom *you* brought out of the land of Egypt"* (emphasis added), not Moses' people, as God had evasively tried to claim in verse 7. In spite of the obvious misbehavior of the Israelites, Moses asks, "O LORD, why does your wrath burn hot against your people?" (v. 11). Since Moses has already heard the rationale for the divine fury in the previous verses, this inquiry is not asking for information. Instead, it is intended to call into question the wisdom of an angry and destructive reaction on the part of God. First, according to Moses, God's reputation is at stake: "Why should the Egyptians say, 'It was with evil intent that he brought them out to kill them in the mountains, and to consume them from the face of the earth'?" (v. 12). Moses appeals to God, "Turn from your fierce wrath; change your mind and do not bring disaster on your people" (v. 12). Otherwise, God's character and essential nature will be perceived as evil and destructive. Second, according to Moses, God's faithfulness to God's promises is at stake: "Remember Abraham, Isaac, and Israel, your servants, how you swore to them by your own self, saying to them, 'I will multiply your descendants like the stars of heaven, and all this land that I have promised I will give to your descendants, and they shall inherit it forever'" (v. 13). If God reneges on God's promises in the past of progeny and land, there will be no grounds for trusting God in the future. In this case, conversation results in the acquiescence of God to the wisdom of Moses: "The LORD changed his mind about the disaster that he planned to bring on his people" (v. 14). This exchange between Moses and God models open and honest conversation between parties committed to seeing to it that not just some but all attitudes, perceptions, and behaviors—and their consequences—are on the table for discussion, clarification, and appropriate action.

Conversation that explores openly and honestly the differences in perception, attitude, and behavior of the parties involved is a frequently attested biblical response to diversity. In and of itself, of course, conversation is no panacea. Rashi interprets Genesis 4:8 in which "Cain said to his brother Abel": "He entered with him into conversation (which would lead to) argument and contention to seek a pretext against him to kill him."[3] The book of Jeremiah expresses on multiple occasions that the deity is no longer inclined to listen, as in 15:1: "Then the LORD said to me: Though Moses and Samuel stood before me, yet my heart would not turn toward this people," and in 11:14: "As for you, do not pray for this people, or lift up a cry or prayer on their behalf, for I will not listen when they call to me in the time of their trouble." In spite of the fact that Jesus is said to have "explained everything in private to his disciples" (Mark 4:34), still there were times that they "did not understand . . . but their hearts were hardened" (6:52). Conversation is clearly no cure-all, but open and honest communication on common ground has the capacity to ground relationships in similarities and solidarity regardless of differences.

LIKE A CHILD

A Sermon on 2 Kings 5:1-14

What are little girls made of? "Sugar and spice and everything nice—that's what little girls are made of." In an enlightened and liberated era such as our own, we know better than to put much stock in such old-fashioned, gender-biased adages, not to mention the fact that experience has introduced at least some of us to any number of diminutive preadolescent females who seem to be composed of anything but "sugar and spice and everything nice." Even so, we might be surprised to see in this morning's Old Testament lectionary passage a child of an entirely different mettle than in the nursery rhyme. We never learn her name or anything about her other than what we read in 2 Kings 5:2-4. But from what we do learn about her in these three verses, I want to suggest an alternative adage to characterize this unnamed *naʿărâ qĕṭannâ*, this "little girl" from the land of Israel: Nails and gold and everything bold— that's what this girl is made of.

There is a cast of powerful people in the fifth chapter of 2 Kings. There is Naaman, the Syrian general. There is the king of Syria and the king of Israel. And there is the prophet Elisha, the wonder-working successor to Elijah in the company of the prophets in Israel. Those of us who see the world through adult eyes may be quick to assume that we can learn the most from the most powerful people in the story. It's a common mistake that we adults make. But in point of fact, it's the unnamed, diminutive preadolescent female from whom we can learn the most. So much so, in fact, that I am inclined to make the rather outlandish suggestion that no less a preacher and teacher than Jesus of Nazareth had this little girl in mind when he is quoted in Mark 10:15 and Luke 18:17 as having said, "I assure you that whoever does not receive the Kingdom of God like a child will never enter it" (GNT).

In most Christian teaching and preaching down through the centuries, we have been taught that when Jesus said, "like a child," he was talking about something like children's trustful simplicity, their naive humility, or their innocent obedience. To tell you the truth, most sermons I've heard on those words of Jesus have made me wonder if the people who preached them had ever spent much time at all with children. Certainly not with my children—or most of yours either, from what I know. Most of those Sunday school lessons have made me wonder if the people who wrote them had ever read the stories in the Bible about children and youth. In those stories, we see youngsters behaving quite differently than in the sermons and Sunday school lessons. For example, it was David, the youngest of Jesse's sons and "just a boy," who stepped forward in a crisis to say of the warrior Goliath, "I will go and fight him" (1 Samuel 17:32 GNT). Then there was Mary, in her teens and unwed, who responded no less courageously, "Here am I, the servant of the Lord; let it be with me according to your word" (Luke 1:38). And then there was Mary's son Jesus, who at twelve years old amazed the teachers in the temple with "his understanding and his answers" to their questions (Luke 2:47). When we look at the children portrayed in Scripture, we see qualities that amaze and confound the adults around them and sometimes even put the adults to shame. And in this morning's Scripture passage we see one of those children, a girl of nails and gold and everything bold.

As outlandish as the suggestion is that Jesus had this little girl in mind, it is not entirely unimaginable. Luke 4:27 tells us that when people in Jesus' hometown of Nazareth began to praise a sermon he had just preached in the synagogue, he reminded them of this story of "a little maid from the land of Israel" (2 Kings 5:2 RSV). Jesus said, "There were many people suffering from a dreaded skin disease who lived in Israel during the time of the prophet Elisha; yet not one of them was healed, but only Naaman the Syrian" (GNT). The Gospel of Luke goes on to tell us that when the good religious people of Nazareth heard these words of Jesus, they became so angry that they turned against him on the spot and wanted to kill him. Syrians, you see, have never been particularly popular in Israel. Along with the Philistines and the Moabites, the Syrians were singled out for animosity as the most bitter of Israel's historic enemies. So when Jesus mentioned the healing of Naaman the Syrian, he so infuriated his audience that their praises turned to a murderous rage. Now, Luke's Gospel doesn't mention the little girl of nails and gold and everything bold, but it was because of her that Naaman the Syrian was healed. Without her initiative there would be no story to tell of Elisha healing the Syrian general. And so I am suggesting that Jesus was thinking of her—or someone very much like her—when he said, "I assure you that whoever does not receive the Kingdom of God like a child will never enter it" (Mark 10:15 GNT). Nails and gold and everything bold.

I say, "nails," because she was "tough as." Consider what we know about this girl's situation. She was an Israelite captive who Syrian raiders had carried away from her village. Naaman the general must have selected her as part of the spoils of war to give to his wife as a household slave. So when this girl suggests in 2 Kings 5:3 that Naaman could be cured of his disease if only he would pay a visit to "the prophet who lives in Samaria," she reveals an amazing toughness. She reveals that in spite of the terror, misfortune, and dislocation that have come her way, she has not abandoned her confidence in her God or in the religious institutions of her upbringing. How could her faith be so tenacious as to survive and even thrive as a captive in a foreign land instead of a child at home?

Perhaps she remembered the sacred stories that her father had taught her about the time of the judges in Israel and how the people "abandoned the LORD, the God of their ancestors, who had brought them out of the land of Egypt. . . . So the anger of the LORD was kindled against Israel, and he gave them over to plunderers who plundered them, and he sold them into the power of their enemies all around, so that they could no longer withstand their enemies" (Judges 2:12, 14). If she remembered the stories of the judges that her father taught her, she might have concluded that what had happened to her was not because her faith was in vain or because God did not love her, but was instead a consequence of human sin. And in her recognition that sin and disaster sometimes go hand in hand, this little girl could have discovered in herself the toughness she needed to keep the faith, resist despair, and reject cynicism.

Or maybe she recollected the proverbial lessons that her mother had taught her. Maybe she recalled words like these: "Those who trust in their own wits are fools; but those who walk in wisdom come through safely" (Proverbs 28:26). If she remembered those words or others like them that her mother taught her, she might have concluded that what had happened to her was not because her faith was in vain or because God did not love her, but was instead a consequence of human stupidity and foolishness. And in her recognition that stupidity and disaster sometimes go hand in hand, this little girl could have discovered in herself the toughness she needed to keep the faith, resist despair, and reject cynicism.

Or maybe she recalled her grandfather's voice of experience in words akin to what Ecclesiastes wrote: "The race is not to the swift, nor the battle to the strong, nor bread to the wise, nor riches to the intelligent, nor favor to the skillful; but time and chance happen to them all" (Ecclesiastes 9:11-12). If she recollected those words or others like them that her grandfather taught her, she might have concluded that what had happened to her was not because her faith was in vain or because God did not love her, but because time and chance happen to us all. And in her recognition that chance and disaster sometimes go hand in hand, this little girl could have discovered in herself the toughness she needed to keep the faith, resist despair, and reject cynicism.

This "girl from the land of Israel" models for us the toughness and the tenacity of faith that is required for citizenship in the kingdom of God. The author of the book of Revelation understood what it takes when he wrote, "As a follower of Jesus I am your partner in patiently enduring the suffering that comes to those who belong to his Kingdom" (Revelation 1:9 GNT). That's not the kind of talk we like to hear about citizenship in the Kingdom, is it? When is the last time you saw a sign outside a church that read, "Come suffer patiently with us"? That's not a gospel you and I want to hear or preach, much less to live. We buy the triumphant *Christus Victor* who vanquished death and evil, and we sell the Suffering Servant because we want no part of servanthood or suffering—either one. We preach a Christ who conquers, overcomes, protects, and defends us against all comers, a national championship Jesus. And then we find ourselves and our theology utterly unprepared for the adversity that comes our way in life when there is no triumph, only travail; when the losses in our lives pile up and the wins are few and far between at best or evidently all in the past. In adversity, our faith slips away like sand through our fingers, and we fall into despair or cynicism, unlike the girl from the land of Israel who understood what it meant to be a suffering servant of God because she had not sold her soul to a theology of victory and success. Nails, because she was tough as.

Nails and gold. I say "gold" because she had "a heart of." Why it ever occurred to this child to be so astonishingly compassionate as to wish that her captor could be cured of his disease we will never know. Perhaps she is one of the earliest examples of the "Stockholm syndrome" or "capture bonding," as it is also known, in which persons who are held hostage, including prisoners of war, kidnapping victims, battered wives, and abused children, become emotionally attached and intensely loyal to their captors. Or perhaps it wasn't the Stockholm syndrome at all. Perhaps her circumstances as a household slave in the home of a wealthy and pampered Syrian woman was an easier and happier condition than she had known in the home of her rude, impoverished Israelite father who had no good use for a daughter who was no help to him in the fields. Or perhaps it was not her circumstances at all but her character. Maybe she was one of those unusually empathetic children you come across from time to time, that child with a sensitivity to others takes everyone by surprise. We can't get behind the text in front of us to reconstruct her experience and her feelings, but what we can see in the three verses in which she appears is an astonishing compassion that looks right past differences in nationality and religion and disparities in power and wealth to see the commonality of human suffering and need.

Instead of pointing Naaman toward a cure, she could have called down curses on his head. She certainly didn't lack for ammunition. An earlier story in 2 Kings, in which Elisha appears, goes like this: "Elisha left Jericho to go to Bethel, and on the way some boys came out of a town and made fun of him. 'Get out of here, baldy!' they shouted. Elisha turned around, glared at them, and cursed them in the name of the LORD. Then two she-bears came out of the woods and tore forty-two of the boys to pieces" (2 Kings 2:23-24 GNT). As an increasingly balding preacher who is the father of three boys, I have come to have a wicked appreciation for that little story. That's the Elisha she could have thought of when she looked at the man who was responsible for her captivity. But instead, she said, "I wish that my master could go to the prophet who lives in Samaria! He would cure him of his disease." That is astonishing compassion on the part of a victim of conquest and coercion. And it is precisely the compassion that is required for citizenship in the kingdom of God, as Jesus puts it in the Sermon on the Mount: "You have heard that it was said, 'Love your friends, hate your enemies.' But now I tell you: love your enemies and pray for those who persecute you" (Matthew 5:43-44 GNT). That's another piece of the gospel for which it is typically hard to find a practitioner in these days of political, religious, and national partisanship, polemics, and polarization. But we've found one in 2 Kings 5. In the three verses in which she appears, this child exhibits kingdom-of-God compassion for her enemy and oppressor. Nails and gold, because she had a heart of.

Nails and gold and everything bold. I say, "everything bold," because this girl makes an outrageously bold claim on the grace and mercy of God. We have no idea how she knew that Elisha and her God would cure the Syrian general of this disease. Perhaps she had suffered from it herself, or perhaps someone in her family had, or perhaps the reputation of this prophet and his company of healers was so widespread that she needed no personal experience with his gift of healing to think that he would do so. However she knew it—or perhaps only believed or hoped or prayed it— she was outrageously bold in her offer to Naaman. She invited him to avail himself of the health and well-being that were available in her own community. She invited the wolf into the sheepfold, for heaven's sake. And when she did, she made an outrageous claim on the grace and mercy of God by suggesting that God would act to heal an enemy of God's people and a victimizer of one of God's children. Perhaps she remembered the story her grandmother had told her of Abraham playing the "prophet" (Genesis 20:7) by praying to God on behalf of the king of Gerar, Abimelech, who had taken Abraham's wife Sarah for his own. The result of Abraham's prayer, Genesis 20:17 tells us, was that "God healed Abimelech" and Abimelech's entire household. If God would heal King Abimelech who took Sarah from Abraham, then surely God would heal General Naaman who took her from the land of Israel.

She could have rejoiced at Naaman's misery. She could have interpreted his suffering as a judgment from God and a vindication of herself and her people. After all, the skin condition from which he suffered, *měṣōrāʿ* in Hebrew in verse 3, is attested elsewhere in the Old Testament as a punishment from God, as on Miriam the sister of Moses in Numbers 12:10. To see that he has contracted this "dreaded skin disease" could have made her heart leap for joy like the Cuban Americans who celebrated in the streets of Little Havana when Fidel Castro became ill, or like the Palestinians who danced in the streets of Gaza City when the twin towers of the World Trade Center collapsed. She could have rejoiced at the suffering of this one who was responsible for her exile and her servitude, but instead she claimed that God whom she worshiped was every bit as interested in and concerned for Naaman's health and well-being as for her own. And so she made the outrageously bold claim on the grace and mercy of God that if Naaman could but visit the prophet who lived in Samaria, her God would heal him.

Surely you can understand why the good people of Nazareth became so incensed at Jesus when he reminded them of this passage from Scripture that they wanted to ignore because it disrupted their self-possessed religious and national prejudices. A leprous Syrian warrior is healed while Israelite men, women, and children suffer. It made them furious that Jesus proclaimed as "the truth" (Luke 4:25) an understanding of God that insists that God does not discriminate against those whom we despise or detest. In Luke 6, Jesus says:

> If you love those who love you, what credit is that to you? For even sinners love those who love them. If you do good to those who do good to you, what credit is that to you? For even sinners do the same. If you lend to those from whom you hope to receive, what credit is that to you? Even sinners lend to sinners, to receive as much again. But love your enemies, do good, and lend, expecting nothing in return. Your reward will be great, and you will be children of the Most High; for he is kind to the ungrateful and the wicked. Be merciful, just as your Father is merciful. (Luke 6:32-36)

In the end, it's not the sociological imperative—"love your enemies"—that infuriates Jesus' audiences then and now. It's the theological declarative that angers us most: God is "kind to the ungrateful and the wicked," Jesus says, and God is merciful to those whom we count as our enemies. That's the teaching of Jesus that keeps us from becoming citizens in the kingdom of God as Jesus preaches and teaches it because citizenship in the kingdom of God entails worshiping and serving a God who loves even those who do not love God, a God who is good even to those who are not. That's what this "little girl" from the land of Israel understood about God that you and I have not yet been willing to accept and to live by. Nails and gold and everything bold: "Whoever does not receive the Kingdom of God like a child will never enter it" (Mark 10:15 GNT).

> Let us pray. Grant us, O God, that we may be like this child we have met in Scripture who models for us what it takes to enter the kingdom of God: toughness equal to the challenges we face, compassion equal to the challenges faced by others, and boldness equal to the breadth of your grace and mercy, through Jesus Christ our Lord. Amen.

CHAPTER 4

BIBLICAL RESPONSES TO DIVERSITY: COLLABORATION

A seventh biblical response to diversity is *collaboration*, working together across the boundaries of differences in attributes, perspectives, attitudes, and behaviors. This response is epitomized by the "wisdom tradition" in the Bible and throughout the ancient Near East.[1] Biblical and ancient Near Eastern "wisdom literature" exhibits some remarkable similarities in perspective, as well as shared literary genres such as "instructions, proverb collections, dialogues on divine justice and human suffering, pseudo-autobiographies, and philosophical exhortations to a certain way of life."[2] Represented in the Bible primarily in the books of Proverbs, Ecclesiastes, and Job, as well as in numerous isolated passages in other books, the irenic and international perspective of wisdom is depicted in the portrait of Solomon as wisdom's patron *par excellence*:

God gave Solomon very great wisdom, discernment, and breadth of understanding as vast as the sand on the seashore, so that Solomon's wisdom surpassed the wisdom of all the people of the east, and all the wisdom of Egypt. He was wiser than anyone else, wiser than Ethan the Ezrahite, and Heman,

Calcol, and Darda, children of Mahol; his fame spread throughout all the surrounding nations. He composed three thousand proverbs, and his songs numbered a thousand and five. He would speak of trees, from the cedar that is in the Lebanon to the hyssop that grows in the wall; he would speak of animals, and birds, and reptiles, and fish. People came from all the nations to hear the wisdom of Solomon; they came from all the kings of the earth who had heard of his wisdom. (1 Kings 4:29-34)

Clearly, to be "wise" in the biblical tradition entailed much more than either "local knowledge" or sectarian religious doctrine. It included facility in poetry and expertise in flora and fauna (vv. 32-33), and it was measured on an international and cross-cultural—and therefore interfaith—scale (vv. 30-31, 34). Wisdom moved people to cross national, ethnic, and religious boundaries (v. 34).

The capacity of wisdom to cross cultural boundaries is evident in biblical and extrabiblical examples. Excavations at Elephantine in southern Egypt have unearthed Aramaic documents belonging to an Israelite colony there. Dating primarily from the fifth century BCE, the texts include a copy of a collection of wisdom known as "The Words of Ahiqar," who was a "wise scribe" in the Assyrian court of the kings Sennacherib (2 Kings 18:13) and Esarhaddon (2 Kings 19:37).[3] This discovery captures wisdom's geographical and cultural transportability: Assyrian wisdom in an Israelite library in southern Egypt. The collaborative reach of wisdom is also exemplified within the Bible in Proverbs 22:17–24:22. These "words of the wise" (22:17) are an Israelite adaptation of a thirteenth-century Egyptian text, *The Instruction of Amenemopet*.

For example, the question asked in Proverbs 22:20, "Have I not written for you thirty sayings of admonition and knowledge?" makes no sense in its current literary setting in Proverbs, but it is eminently sensible at the close of the collection of Amenemopet's instruction, which is organized into thirty chapters: "See thou these thirty chapters: They entertain; they instruct; They are the foremost of all books."[4] A proverb about riches that disappear quickly, as though they fly away, is adapted from "geese" in *Amenemopet* ("They have made themselves wings like geese And are flown away to the heavens," x.4-5) to an "eagle" in Proverbs 23:5 ("for suddenly it takes wings to itself, flying like an eagle toward heaven").[5] Gagging on one's greed shows up in *Amenemopet* xiv and in Proverbs 23:

> Be not greedy for the property of a poor man,
> Nor hunger for his bread.
> As for the property of a poor man, it is a blocking
>   of the throat,
> It makes a vomiting to the gullet. . . .
> The mouthful of bread (too) great thou swallowest
>   and vomitest up,
> And art emptied of thy good.[6]

> Do not eat the bread of the stingy;
>   do not desire their delicacies;
>   for like a hair in the throat, so are they. . . .
> You will vomit up the little you have eaten,
>   and you will waste your pleasant words. (Proverbs 23:6-8)

Proverbial wisdom encapsulates and inculcates the wisdom of experience, and its ancient proponents recognized that for all its cross-cultural differences, human experience is profoundly similar—similar enough that Egyptian wisdom could be incorporated into the biblical book of Proverbs as easily as Assyrian wisdom could be collected in an Israelite library.

The book of Acts depicts the apostle Paul as following the lead of this widely collaborative vision of ancient Israel's wisdom when he incorporated quotations of a Greek philosopher and a Greek poet into a sermon in Athens: "For 'In him we live and move and have our being'; as even some of your own poets have said, 'For we too are his offspring'" (Acts 17:28). Acts presents Paul as affirming these pagan writers' perspective on God and the relation of all persons to

God. Although the goal of the sermon is undeniably conversion (v. 30), along the way it incorporates insights and
practices from pagan sources, the most remarkable claim
being that the Athenians were already honoring the God
whom Paul was proclaiming at their altar "to an unknown
god" (v. 23). Verses 24-26 reflect the coexistence response to
diversity identified in Deuteronomy 32:8-9, when it asserts
that "the God who made the world and everything in it . . .
made all nations to inhabit the whole earth, and he allotted
the times of their existence and the boundaries of the places
where they would live." However, Acts 17:27 introduces a
decidedly wisdom twist when it depicts human beings as
being in a position to "search for God and perhaps grope for
him and find him—though indeed he is not far from each
one of us." Some commentators have suggested that this depiction of God who is widely accessible to ancient "seekers"
(in contrast to God who is accessible only to those who receive God's self-revelation, for example, at Sinai, in the law,
the prophets, and so forth) is a concession to the perspective
of the Hellenistic audience in Athens. But it is not so much a
concession as it is a connection of the thought-world of first-
century Athens to the wisdom tradition of the Old Testament
and the ancient Near East.

In the wisdom tradition, instruction in the ways of God in
the world did not require travel to sacred sites where religious knowledge was revealed and mediated, nor did it require the services of specialized handlers of revealed
knowledge such as prophets, priests, diviners, and seers. Divine wisdom was understood to be available at home in
"your father's commandment" and in "your mother's teaching" (Proverbs 6:20), as well as widely accessible in the
world for "those who have ears to hear" when the personi-
fied woman Wisdom calls out and raises her voice: "On the
heights, beside the way, at the crossroads she takes her stand;
beside the gates in front of the town, at the entrance of the
portals she cries out" (Proverbs 8:2-3). In the countryside and
in the city, in busy places and in far-flung locations in

between, wisdom is to be found wherever in the world one searches out divine wisdom, which can be acquired by careful observation of nature and society. So, in Proverbs 6, observation of nature illuminates wise character and responsible behavior in the world.

> Go to the ant, you lazybones;
>> consider its ways and be wise.
> Without having any chief or officer or ruler,
> it prepares its food in summer,
>> and gathers its sustenance in harvest.
> How long will you lie there, O lazybones?
>> When will you rise from your sleep?
> A little sleep, a little slumber,
> a little folding of the hands to rest,
> and poverty will come upon you like a robber,
>> and want, like an armed warrior. (Proverbs 6:6-11)

Here, careful observation of the way the divinely constituted order of the natural world works leads to wise behavior.

The saying of Jesus in Matthew 6:26-30 exemplifies observational wisdom, even as it counters the call for antlike incessant activity driven by the fear of scarcity in Proverbs 6:

> Look at the birds of the air; they neither sow nor reap nor gather into barns, and yet your heavenly Father feeds them. . . . Consider the lilies of the field, how they grow; they neither toil nor spin, yet I tell you, even Solomon in all his glory was not clothed like one of these. But if God so clothes the grass of the field, which is alive today and tomorrow is thrown into the oven, will he not much more clothe you—you of little faith?

Careful observations of the natural and social order need not arrive at the same conclusion in order to be wise, as the juxtaposed proverbs in Proverbs 26:4-5 illustrate.

> Do not answer fools according to their folly,
>> or you will be a fool yourself.

> Answer fools according to their folly,
>   or they will be wise in their own eyes.

In no dimension of human experience with which we are currently familiar is it possible to carry out these two instructions simultaneously. Still, the "wisdom of experience" includes both of these proverbs because they each speak truthfully: there are times when the wisest thing a person can do is walk away instead of stooping to a foolish level by entering the conversation, debate, or argument, and there are times when a person has a responsibility to interject wisdom into a conversation dominated by foolishness and error. Similarly, the font of wisdom who says, "Whoever is not against you is for you" (Luke 9:50) can also say, "Whoever is not with me is against me" (Luke 11:23). The truly "wise" are those who can discern rightly the occasions on which the one wisdom or the other applies, depending on the content and the context of the conversation, controversy, or conflict.

The instruction concerning adultery in Proverbs 6 further illustrates the observational and analytical ground of wisdom. Revealed knowledge, as exhibited in the Ten Commandments, which God gave to the people of Israel at Mount Sinai, says succinctly of adultery, "Thou shalt not" (Exodus 20:14; Deuteronomy 5:18 KJV). For wisdom, however, one is not dependent on heavenly instruction; earthly instruction and observation of human nature and social realities leads one to an appropriate attitude and wise behavior:

> The reproofs of discipline are the way of life,
> to preserve you from the wife of another,
>   from the smooth tongue of the adulteress.
> Do not desire her beauty in your heart,
>   and do not let her capture you with her eyelashes;
> for a prostitute's fee is only a loaf of bread,
>   but the wife of another stalks a man's very life.
>   (Proverbs 6:23b-26)

Wisdom's counsel acknowledges the temptations of "the smooth tongue" (a double entendre, if ever there was one!), desirable "beauty," and captivating "eyelashes." It is, after all, human nature to be tempted. But instead of invoking the divine prohibition against adultery as the answer to temptation, verse 26 offers a brief "cost-benefit analysis" based on the observation of social realities. "Count the cost," it counsels: a prostitute costs a lot less. After a pair of rhetorical questions suggestive of the dangers of close proximity to heat and which invite a No! from the reader instead of from God, the cost-benefit analysis returns by suggesting that the consequences of thievery are lighter than those of adultery.

> Thieves are not despised who steal only
> to satisfy their appetite when they are hungry.
> Yet if they are caught, they will pay sevenfold;
> they will forfeit all the goods of their house.
> But he who commits adultery has no sense;
> he who does it destroys himself.
> He will get wounds and dishonor,
> and his disgrace will not be wiped away.
> For jealousy arouses a husband's fury,
> and he shows no restraint when he takes revenge.
> He will accept no compensation,
> and refuses a bribe no matter how great.
>
> (Proverbs 6:30-35)

Wisdom's pragmatic counsel to count the cost by observing and understanding social realities is reflected in Jesus' teaching in the Gospel of Luke, complete with "putting the question" that engages the audience in the discourse:

> For which of you, intending to build a tower, does not first sit down and estimate the cost, to see whether he has enough to complete it? Otherwise, when he has laid a foundation and is not able to finish, all who see it will begin to ridicule him, saying, "This fellow began to build and was not able to finish." Or what king, going out to wage war against another king, will not sit down first and consider whether he is able

with ten thousand to oppose the one who comes against him with twenty thousand? If he cannot, then, while the other is still far away, he sends a delegation and asks for the terms of peace. (Luke 14:28-32)

Instead of recommending consultation with a diviner, seer, or prophet who will ascertain "the will of God" concerning building the tower or waging the war, Jesus' instruction points to the capacity of the reader to "figure it out," quite literally, by counting the cost of the behavior before engaging in it.

Wisdom in antiquity is typically practical, pragmatic counsel that leads to wise living and worldly success. However, to treat the ancient Near Eastern and biblical wisdom tradition as a merely materialistic pragmatism is to shine light on only one portion of wisdom's field. To "speak of the whole" where wisdom is concerned, it is necessary to recognize that the ultimate validation of the wisdom of experience is not that "it works," but that *it works consistently with the movement of divine, cosmic wisdom in the created order*. The book of Proverbs insists repeatedly that "the fear of [awe of, reverence for, worship of] the LORD is the beginning of wisdom" (Proverbs 9:10).[7] This claim is not grounded in private, personal piety. Instead, it is anchored in the wisdom tradition's understanding that both the natural world and the social systems of human interaction operate according to principles of divine cosmic wisdom established in creation. Jeremiah 10:12 captures the idea in a hymnic fragment: "It is he who made the earth by his power, *who established the world by his wisdom*" (emphasis added). The collaborative role of wisdom in creation receives its most extensive treatment in the Old Testament in Proverbs 8, where woman Wisdom's hymn claims:

The LORD created me at the beginning of his work,
    the first of his acts of long ago.
Ages ago I was set up,
    at the first, before the beginning of the earth.

When there were no depths I was brought forth,
    when there were no springs abounding with water.
Before the mountains had been shaped,
    before the hills, I was brought forth—
when he had not yet made earth and fields,
    or the world's first bits of soil.
When he established the heavens, I was there,
    when he drew a circle on the face of the deep,
when he made firm the skies above,
    when he established the fountains of the deep,
when he assigned to the sea its limit,
    so that the waters might not transgress his command,
when he marked out the foundations of the earth,
    then I was beside him, like a master worker;
and I was daily his delight,
    rejoicing before him always,
rejoicing in his inhabited world
    and delighting in the human race. (vv. 22-31)

Wisdom is at work and at play in the created order from the very beginning, collaborating with God in creative activity and in delight at its outcome.

This passage from Proverbs 8 draws back the curtain on the Jewish background in the wisdom tradition of the remarkable claim of the prologue to the Gospel of John, "In the beginning was the Word, and the Word was with God, and the Word was God. He was in the beginning with God. All things came into being through him, and without him not one thing came into being" (John 1:1-3). The Word at work in creation is none other than "the power of God and *the wisdom of God*" who is Christ, according to Paul in 1 Corinthians 1:24 (emphasis added). What John and Paul assert theologically, the Gospel of Luke affirms biographically, when the gospel tradition observes of Jesus, "The child grew and became strong, *filled with wisdom*," and "Jesus *increased in wisdom*" (Luke 2:40, 52, emphasis added). In Matthew's Gospel, it is a simultaneously biographical and theological question asked in his hometown of Nazareth,

"Where did this man get this wisdom and these deeds of power?" (Matthew 13:54). The biblical wisdom tradition is pragmatic and practical, and at the same time it is inherently theological and cosmological as well.

At the outset of his attempt to address the "divisions" and "quarrels" in the church at Corinth over competing loyalties to different leaders (1 Corinthians 1:10-16), Paul engages in an extended discourse on wisdom. As is wisdom's manner, he begins his treatment of the matter at hand with a set of rhetorical questions intended to elicit a no from his audience: "Has Christ been divided? Was Paul crucified for you? Or were you baptized in the name of Paul?" Paul then disparages worldly wisdom, as is evident from these selected statements:

> For the message about the cross is foolishness to those who are perishing, but to us who are being saved it is the power of God. For it is written,
> "I will destroy the wisdom of the wise,
> and the discernment of the discerning I will thwart"
> [Isaiah 29:14].
> Where is the one who is wise? . . . Has God not made foolish the wisdom of the world? For since, in the wisdom of God, the world did not know God through wisdom, God decided, through the foolishness of our proclamation, to save those who believe. For Jews demand signs and Greeks desire wisdom, but we proclaim Christ crucified, a stumbling block to Jews and foolishness to Gentiles. . . . For God's foolishness is wiser than human wisdom, and God's weakness is stronger than human strength. . . . Not many of you were wise by human standards. . . . But God chose what is foolish in the world to shame the wise. . . . I did not come proclaiming the mystery of God to you in lofty words or wisdom. . . . My speech and my proclamation were not with plausible words of wisdom, but with a demonstration of the Spirit and of power, so that your faith might rest not on human wisdom but on the power of God. (1 Corinthians 1:18–2:5)

Paul's contrast between what is wise and what is foolish is a typical wisdom conceit. However, Paul is clearly grounding the case he is making in *revelation* rather than in *wisdom*, and he goes on to say that this *revealed wisdom* is not at all self-evident in the world.

> Yet among the mature we do speak wisdom, though it is not a wisdom of this age or of the rulers of this age, who are doomed to perish. But we speak God's wisdom, secret and hidden, which God decreed before the ages for our glory. . . . These things God has revealed to us through the Spirit; for the Spirit searches everything, even the depths of God. . . . And we speak of these things in words not taught by human wisdom but taught by the Spirit, interpreting spiritual things to those who are spiritual. (1 Corinthians 2:6-7, 10, 13)

In addition to serving as a seedbed for Gnostic heresies for centuries to come, Paul's depiction of divine wisdom as something "secret and hidden," revealed only to some "through the Spirit," clearly departs from the mainstream of the ancient wisdom tradition reflected in the Old Testament and elsewhere in the New Testament.

The extent of this departure is evident in the fact that four of the six Old Testament passages that Paul quotes or at least alludes to in this segment of his letter are not "wisdom passages" at all (though they may include the word "wisdom") but are selected from the prophets.[8] Richard Hays has aptly described Paul's approach as reflecting the development of "the apocalyptic dimension of divine wisdom." He writes:

> Paul's language is indigenous to Jewish apocalyptic thought, where the "mysteries" concern the concealed will of God, which is to play itself out in the historical unfolding of the eschatological events of judgment and salvation. These mysteries are revealed to the elect though [sic] the mediation of the prophet or seer.[9]

This is wisdom transposed into an entirely different key.[10] Still, it is instructive that Paul considers reflection on the nature of wisdom—practical and theological, pragmatic and cosmological—to be the first move in addressing the tensions associated with a diversity of attitudes, perception, and behavior in the church.

Wisdom is portrayed quite differently as an essential characteristic of leadership in the church in a story about the resolution of a conflict involving diversity in Acts 6:1-6. As "the disciples were increasing in number," they were also increasing in ethnic, cultural, and social diversity, resulting in tensions in the community. The catalyst for conflict between "Hellenists," probably Greek-speaking, Diaspora-reared believers, and "Hebrews," probably Aramaic-speaking natives of Palestine, was the Hellenists' perception that "their widows were being neglected in the daily distribution of food" (Acts 6:1). The apostles, all "Hebrews," called "the whole community" together to discuss the matter. They conveniently sidestepped the charge of ethnic discrimination by interpreting the issue in terms of a shortage of their time and the breadth of their responsibilities: "It is not right that we should neglect the word of God in order to wait on tables" (v. 2). So they suggest that the Hellenists, "Select from among yourselves seven men of good standing, full of the Spirit and of wisdom, whom we may appoint to this task" (v. 3). "What they said," we are told, "pleased the whole community," and seven new leaders, native Greek-speakers judging by their names in verse 5, were chosen. Collaboration replaced conflict as Hellenists and Hebrews alike worked together across ethnic and cultural boundaries that had threatened to divide the community.

Collaboration across ethnic, cultural, and even religious boundaries plays a critical role at several key junctures in the Bible. In Exodus 18:13-26, the "priest of Midian," Jethro (v. 1), Moses' father-in-law, proposed to Moses a judicial process that would reduce the burden on Moses, and "Moses listened to his father-in-law and did all that he had said" (v. 24). When the book of Deuteronomy narrates the establishment of this process a second time, it omits any mention of the Midianite contribution to the Israelite judiciary

(Deuteronomy 1:9-18), but Exodus asserts that it originated in a cross-cultural and interfaith collaboration of the Midianite Jethro with the Israelite Moses.

According to 1 Kings, when Solomon set out "to build a house for the name of the LORD my God" (5:5), he sought access to cedars from Lebanon and the assistance of Phoenician woodsmen in procuring them. He sent word to Hiram, king of Tyre: "My servants will join your servants . . . for you know that there is no one among us who knows how to cut timber like the Sidonians" (v. 6). And not timber alone, but stonecutting also, according to verse 18: "So Solomon's builders and Hiram's builders and the Giblites [inhabitants of the Phoenician port city later named Byblos] did the stonecutting and prepared the timber and the stone to build the house." The finishing touches were applied by a Phoenician artisan named Hiram (no relation to the king) who is characterized as "full of skill, intelligence, and knowledge in working bronze. He came [from Tyre] to King Solomon, and did all his work" adorning the temple in Jerusalem (7:14). The account in Kings is careful not to connect the dots between this Phoenician activity in Jerusalem with another Phoenician who will play a prominent role later in the book, Queen Jezebel, the wife of King Ahab of Israel (1 Kings 16, 18-19, 21). Nevertheless, Kings portrays the construction of Solomon's temple to the Lord as a cross-cultural and interfaith collaborative effort between Israelites and Phoenicians. When the temple is rebuilt in Jerusalem after the exile, the services of "Sidonians and Tyrians" are once more required, this time along with the official patronage of "King Cyrus of Persia," according to Ezra 3:7. The book of Ezra goes so far as to claim that the size and design of the second temple were stipulated by Cyrus and that the cost of construction "be paid from the royal treasury" of Persia (Ezra 6:3-4). Ezra claims that a later edict from King Darius required that the cost of finishing the structure and of the daily sacrifices and offerings is to be paid out of the provincial revenues administered from Samaria. According to the Bible, then, the second temple and its daily worship were a collaborative effort of Phoenicians, Persians, and Israelite returnees from the exile, working together across the boundaries of differences in attributes, perspectives, attitudes, and behaviors.

Ironically, then, the construction and the reconstruction of the actual temple in Jerusalem reflect an entirely different picture than the theological sectarianism of the metaphorical temple in 2 Corinthians 6:14–7:1.

> For what partnership is there between righteousness and lawlessness? Or what fellowship is there between light and darkness? What agreement does Christ have with Beliar? Or what does a believer share with an unbeliever? What agreement has the temple of God with idols? For we are the temple of the living God; as God said,
> "I will live in them and walk among them,
> and I will be their God,
> and they shall be my people.
> Therefore come out from them,
> and be separate from them, says the Lord,
> and touch nothing unclean;
> then I will welcome you,
> and I will be your father,
> and you shall be my sons and daughters,
> says the Lord Almighty."
> Since we have these promises, beloved, let us cleanse ourselves from every defilement of body and of spirit, making holiness perfect in the fear of God.

Had this attitude that denies any common ground or basis for collaboration between "believer" and "unbeliever" prevailed in ancient Israel, the temple in Jerusalem could not have been built, nor could it have been rebuilt after the exile. So when Paul puts the question to the Corinthian congregation, "Do you not know that you are God's temple and that God's Spirit dwells in you?" (1 Corinthians 3:16), the collaborative response to diversity looks beyond the fearful, fault-finding pettiness of sectarianism and exclusivism to Solomon's expansive welcome to the temple of the sinner

(1 Kings 8:31), the afflicted (8:38-39), and the foreigner (8:41-43).

When Moses welcomed the contribution to the Israelite judiciary of his Midianite father-in-law, when Solomon employed Phoenician artisans in the construction of the Jerusalem temple, when Proverbs appropriated Egyptian wisdom, and when Paul incorporated Greek poetry and philosophy in his preaching, to point out only a few salient examples, collaboration occurred across boundaries of attributes, attitudes, perceptions, and behavior. Not surprisingly, then, the apostle Paul was able to speak a surprisingly universal benedictory word late in his letter to the church in Philippi: "Finally, beloved, whatever is true, whatever is honorable, whatever is just, whatever is pure, whatever is pleasing, whatever is commendable, if there is any excellence and if there is anything worthy of praise, think about these things" (Philippians 4:8).

Throughout the Old and New Testaments, a wide variety of biblical responses are attested, including attempts to annihilate differences, to live with them, to suppress them, to transform them into similarities, to look past them to act compassionately, to converse openly about them, and to learn from them and incorporate them into the way of wisdom and biblical faith and practice. As the last three chapters have shown, "teaching the whole Bible instead of just part of it" is a much more extensive enterprise than was implied at the beginning of chapter 2 by either my conversation partner's admonition to "make like Joshua" or my own affirmation of "following Jesus." At the very least, we now must ask, "Which Joshua?" Is it the Joshua who "left no one remaining, but utterly destroyed all that breathed" (Joshua 10:40)? Or is it the Joshua who stood up to the angry mob of his own people in defense of the indigenous Gibeonites, with the result that he "saved them from the Israelites; and they did not kill them" (Joshua 9:26)? Similarly, we must now ask, "Which Jesus?" The Jesus who comes in power as the bloody messianic warrior (Revelation 19), the Jesus who counseled coexistence with Caesar (Mark 12:17), the Jesus who required new birth of a Pharisee (John 3:7), or the Jesus who initiated a conversation out of his own need with a stranger at a well (John 4:7)?

And finally, the question that someone inevitably raises is, "But which of these responses to diversity is *the right one*?" The Bible itself neither poses nor answers that question, and its silence is instructive. The quest for one and only one attitude, perception, or behavior that must be authorized as the right, one over against all others is itself an indication of a prior assumption that diversity equals or at least contains error while uniformity equals truth. One may as well ask, "Which one, the Father, the Son, or the Holy Spirit, is the right one manifestation of God?" On this question, the church has historically maintained that insisting on one and only one is not truth but heresy. Similarly, "teaching the whole Bible and not just part of it" requires bringing to our encounter with Scripture the same interpretive savvy that we bring to our reflection on the Trinity. There is more truth in all of the responses together than there is in any one of them alone. After all, Proverbs 26:4 offers wise counsel in some cases, while Proverbs 26:5 is wise in others. Together, they offer more wisdom than either does alone. Pick one and only one if you wish, but the proverbial "voice of experience" suggests that you will be far better prepared to deal with the challenges that you will face if you hold on to both.

In the next two chapters, the questions turn from responses to diversity evident in Scripture to responding to diversity in the current context.

THE NARROW GATE

A Sermon on Matthew 7:12-13

Every November in the United States we observe a national holiday that originated in the capacity of two diverse groups of people to engage each other with compassion and hospitality. The origin of Thanksgiving Day in 1621 is a fascinating moment in American religious history. You know the popular picture: "pilgrims," wearing black hats and shoes with big buckles and carrying blunderbusses, gathered around a table with "Indians," wearing feathered headdresses and deerskin and carrying bows and arrows. It's a cartoon image, of course—a caricature. But the obvious diversity of the people at the table in that cartoon should call our attention to that first Thanksgiving as an object lesson of the best—and of the worst—of which we are capable in our encounter with people of other cultures and other religions.

In the winter of 1620–21, a non-Christian "New World" majority acted compassionately to save a small and struggling "Old World" Christian minority from starving to death. The following autumn, the surviving Europeans invited the locals to participate in the Europeans' traditional harvest festival. The invitation was a gesture of thanks by the Christians for the non-Christians' compassionate action and hospitality to strangers that had saved the Christians' lives the previous winter. When the Native Americans accepted the invitation of the Europeans, that harvest festival celebrated in 1621 became a cross-cultural and interfaith moment for the history books—the history-of-religion books in particular. In the centuries since then, however, the story of that harvest festival has also become a cautionary tale, because from the vantage point of history we can see that in return for having been saved from starvation, the Christian minority, when it became the majority, made like Joshua and drove the native minority from the land of their living, farming, hunting, and burying, as the newcomers conquered, crusaded, and colonized their way across it. The origin of Thanksgiving Day stands as a reminder of the principles of compassionate action and hospitality to strangers that are ingrained in all of the world's enduring religions, but its aftermath stands as a monument to the insidious temptations that ethnocentrism and totalitarianism are to religious majorities, even those who once were a minority. Thanksgiving reminds us of the best of which we are capable, and it reminds us of the worst. Every enduring religion has the power to bring out the best in people and organizations and institutions. And every enduring religion has the capacity to pervert people and organizations and institutions. In different religious traditions, the particulars and the perversions vary, but the principle is the same. We must each and every one choose wisely and well in the practice of our faith, because in all of our traditions there is the power to bring out the best, and there is the capacity to pervert.

One Wednesday evening, I was talking with a friend who was bemoaning the outcome of our national elections the day before. I recognized immediately that I was in the presence of an endangered species in the state of South Carolina, the rarely sighted and frequently depressed Democrat. But he said something that made me realize that his malaise ran deeper than merely being on the losing side of yet another state and national election. "Whatever happened to the squishy middle?" he lamented. "Where has the squishy middle gone?" I bit my tongue and refrained from pointing to his waistline and saying, "I believe it has settled about your belt." I didn't say that. You had to be careful what you said to a depressed Democrat in those days. But what he said made immediate sense as a commentary on the religious climate in our nation, in our world, and in our churches. In the current religious climate, we are at a loss to find a center. Among my own Baptists, among my mother's and my middle brother's Lutherans, among my younger brother's Episcopalians, among my grandmother's Roman Catholics, among my alma mater's Presbyterians, and among my publisher's Methodists, there are no "centers" of any size or substance that we can recognize. And Christians are not alone. Other religions are facing the same challenge. The political and religious polarization we can see within Christianity has its parallels in Judaism, Islam, Hinduism, and even Buddhism, surprisingly enough. In many of the enduring religions around the world, in the words of William Butler Yeats's poem "The Second Coming": "Things fall apart; the center cannot hold. . . . The best lack all conviction, while the worst / Are full of passionate intensity."[1]

The time has come to acknowledge that there is no longer a place in any of our faith traditions for a "squishy middle." In our time, the only middle that is possible is what the eminent observer of the American religious landscape Martin Marty has recently called the "hard middle."[2] There is a wide road of partisanship, polemics, and polarization on the right and on the left, and there is but a narrow road of conversation and collaboration in "the hard middle." That being the case, I want to suggest to you that it is time to issue a new call to enter through "the narrow gate" of which Jesus of Nazareth speaks in Matthew 7:13. For wide and easy is the road that leads to death, to partisanship, polemics, and polarization, but "the gate is narrow and the road is hard" that leads to life, compassion, hospitality, conversation, and collaboration, "and there are few who find it" (Matthew 7:13-14).

If that take on the narrow gate and the hard road sounds a bit off the beaten track to you, then you might be no less surprised to hear that in Matthew's Gospel this saying of Jesus about the easy road that leads to destruction and the hard road that leads to life is attached to another well-known saying of Jesus that in one form or another is attested nearly universally in the enduring religions of our world: "In everything do to others as you would have them do to you" (v. 12). Set side by side in the gospel tradition, the "golden rule" and the "narrow gate" interpret each other.

In the winter of 1620 and 1621, a non-Christian majority living in this land stepped through the narrow gate and on to the hard road to provide for a starving, Christian minority by doing to others as they would have had them do if the big-buckled shoe had been on the other foot. And in the autumn of 1621, a Christian minority stepped through the narrow gate and onto the hard road to invite the non-Christian majority to dinner as a gesture of gratitude, doing to others as they would have had them do if the deerskin moccasin had been on the other foot. It's a wonderful image, this act of coming to the table together. But the sad truth is that the compassion and hospitality of these diverse folk did not lead to lasting conversation and collaboration. In the end, these historic cartoon characters were unable to cultivate the sustained and habitual behavior that builds strong and lasting relationships between people with fundamentally different perspectives and deeply divergent convictions. So the first great American interfaith encounter became a dead end that has left an ambiguous legacy. Today, the national holiday that commemorates that first American interfaith harvest festival has become a platform for a breed of Christian totalitarianism that willfully denies or ignorantly overlooks the interfaith origins of Thanksgiving.

To counteract this perversion of history and of the history of religion in this land, the practitioners of today's enduring religions in America must come to the table together not only at Thanksgiving but often enough throughout the year to ensure that we move from the codependency of hosts and guests to the healthy interdependence of equal partners at the table. We must cultivate one another's company frequently enough that those who were once welcomed as strangers become friends, and those who were once treated compassionately as needy become compatriots in the common good. We have much to learn from one another and much to teach one another. To arrive at the common good together, we must reroute ourselves from the wide and easy road that leads to partisanship, polemics, and polarization to take instead the difficult path where "the gate is narrow and the road is hard" that leads to continuing conversation and sustained collaboration where in everything, we do to others as we would have them do to us.

Those of us who have embarked on that road have discovered along the way kindred spirits and soul mates, compatriots from families and faith perspectives so different from our own that we could not have made them up in our wildest imaginations, and yet so similar to us that we have seen ourselves and our own faith reflected in them. Whether we succeed or fail on the narrow road that is epitomized in the Golden Rule will depend in the end not on how well we get along with one another in the "hard middle"; it will depend instead on how effectively we build bridges of conversation and collaboration to our respective partisan, polemical, and polarizing coreligionists on the wide roads to the right and to the left of us.

So in our churches, our communities, our nation, and our world, when we are finished giving thanks for the hospitality and compassion we have experienced in one another's company, and for the kindred spirits and soul mates we have discovered along the way, it is time to step through the narrow gate again, back on to the hard road where we must build as many bridges as we can to and from it. There in the hard middle, we will answer the call of the enduring religions of our world: to do in everything to others—even to the partisan, the polemical, and the polarizing—as we would have them do to us. The gate is narrow, the road is hard, and we have bridges to build. I'll see you out there.

CHAPTER 5

DIVERSITY LEADERSHIP: QUESTIONS OF CULTURE

Whatever else they may show, the variety of biblical responses to diversity in the last three chapters reveal the considerable degree to which most combatants in the current culture wars in the church have been guilty of proof-texting and cherry-picking to validate their own assumptions and support their partisan arguments about how individuals and congregations should respond to the challenges of diversity in our time. The result has been, to return to Donald Phillip Verene's image, lamplight in the darkness instead of sunlight on the field.[1] To move beyond the impasse of unexamined assumptions and well-rehearsed arguments, it is necessary, as Verene insists, to proceed by putting questions. This chapter follows the lead of three questions that identify aspects of congregational culture that are crucial to redemptive and effective diversity leadership: the root image of the church, its mission, and congregational requirements. As R. Roosevelt Thomas Jr. points out, "Responses to diversity aren't made in a vacuum. They take place within communities."[2] Thus, the greatest challenge for diversity leadership is the fact that "diversity efforts often succeed or fail based on the impact of the organization's culture."[3]

IS IT NOT WRITTEN?

In Mark 11:17, Jesus of Nazareth lays claim to a centuries-old image of the temple in Jerusalem that expresses a core assumption about its purpose and its constituency. Citing Isaiah 56:7, Jesus asks, "Is it not written, 'My house shall be called a house of prayer for all the nations'?" After citing this core image, he offers the following critique: "But you have made it a den of robbers." In the Gospel of John, the issue of Jesus' discontent is identified more broadly when Jesus demands, "Stop making my Father's house a marketplace!" (John 2:16). Is the temple a "house of prayer" or a commercial venture? Does it exist to benefit consumers and those who profit from them or "all the nations"? The question of the temple's root image that Jesus puts to his audience is a reminder that core assumptions, which are typically unexamined, and prevailing language, which is seldom subjected to scrutiny, exert a significant influence on how organizations and institutions function, including how diversity is perceived and addressed.

Organizational culture is shaped in large part by what Thomas calls "core cultural assumptions, or roots" that determine the organization's "behavior with respect to diversity issues."[4] Cultural assumptions are expressed in the prevailing language, images, or metaphors used to characterize the organization. One "core image" that Thomas characterizes as "extremely common—and extremely destructive" is the metaphor of "family."[5] According to Thomas, this root metaphor leads to "a paternalistic climate" in which leaders "take on parental roles" and all others are treated like children. Thomas writes: "Implicit in this scenario . . . is that sons will inherit the business, daughters should stick to doing the . . . dishes, and Uncle Deadwood deserves to stay around regardless of his performance." The "family" root metaphor encourages "a rigid definition of loyalty as childlike obedience and emulation."[6] As popular and evocative as the metaphor of family may be for the church, it suffers from at least two significant shortcomings: it is unbiblical, and it is an organizational fallacy.

New Testament writers do not speak of the church as a "family," no doubt in part because early Jewish and Greco-Roman "family values" frequently conflicted with "Gospel values." This conflict is evident in several of the most disconcerting sayings of Jesus in the Gospels. In the Gospel of Matthew, Jesus says:

> For I have come to set a man against his father, and a daughter against her mother, and a daughter-in-law against her mother-in-law; and one's foes will be members of one's own household. Whoever loves father or mother more than me is not worthy of me; and whoever loves son or daughter more than me is not worthy of me. (Matthew 10:35-37)

The Lukan version of this disconcerting saying is even more categorical: "Whoever comes to me and does not hate father and mother, wife and children, brothers and sisters, yes, and even life itself, cannot be my disciple" (Luke 14:26). When it comes to family, the Jesus of the Gospels has a very different focus from today's "family values" culture. His response to the would-be follower who asked for time to attend to his family obligation in regard to his father's funeral is cold and categorical: "Follow me, and let the dead bury their own dead" (Matthew 8:22). In a diatribe against the religious authorities, Jesus effectively lops off the head of the household when he says: "And call no one your father on earth, for you have one Father—the one in heaven" (Matthew 23:9). In other words, the typical structure of the family of Jesus' day in which the father was the authority to whom all others answered is not an acceptable model for the community of his followers. Indeed, Jesus' call is to abandon one's family and its patriarchal head, as Matthew 4:22 specifically states in the response of Simon and Andrew: "Immediately they left the boat *and their father*, and followed him" (emphasis added). The breadth of the abandonment is articulated in the exchange between Peter and Jesus in Luke 18:28-30: "Then Peter said, 'Look, we have left our homes and followed you.' And he said to them, 'Truly I tell you, there is no one who has left house or wife or brothers or parents or children, for the sake of the kingdom of God, who will not get back very much more in this age, and in the age to come eternal life.'" Finally, when Jesus is informed that "his mother and his brothers" (Mark 3:31) have arrived where he is teaching, he rebuffs their approach by announcing that he does not recognize the validity or the authority of the kinship relations of family. Instead, it is the free and voluntary association of those who align themselves with "the will of God" (Mark 3:35) or who "hear the word of God and do it" (Luke 8:21) who constitute "my brother and sister and mother" (Mark 3:35). With such family-unfriendly words of their Lord ringing in their ears, it would have been unthinkable for New Testament writers to adopt the root image of the "family" for the church.

Unfortunately, the consistency of the New Testament in its avoidance of family as a root image for the church is sometimes obscured by a tendency toward sloppy paraphrasing on the part of modern translators. In Galatians 1:2, the NRSV departs from Paul's cohort of "all the brothers" to introduce instead the sociologically erroneous paraphrase, "all the members of God's *family*" (NIV: "all the brothers"). Paraphrase is sometimes desirable and occasionally even necessary to produce a readable and culturally sensitive translation. This one, however, sacrifices the sociological and theological legitimacy of Paul's language to accommodate the whims of the culture at large or the translators or both. In Galatians 6:10, "the *family* of faith" in the NRSV and NIV replaces Paul's "household," a broader and more diverse sociological unit than the "family." The "*family* of believers" in the NRSV in 1 Peter 2:17 misconstrues an unusual Greek noun constructed from the same root as the word *brother* (NIV: "brotherhood of believers"). The "*family* of God" in the NIV in 1 Peter 4:17 is a substitute for "the household of God" (NRSV). If Paul had wanted to say "family" in these passages, he certainly could have. But he did not.[7]

Instead of "family," the biblical root image of the church is the "assembly," the *ekklēsia,* the Greek word translated "church" in the New Testament. *Ekklēsia* is the word used in the Septuagint (the Greek translation of the Jewish Bible from the fourth century BCE) for the Hebrew word *qāhāl,* "assembly" or "congregation," the "called community." In this root image, the church is the "mixed crowd" (Exodus 12:38) called out of oppression and into the covenantal presence of God at Mount Sinai (Deuteronomy 5:22). This called community includes many households and families; it is a "people of the LORD" (Deuteronomy 27:9), not a "family." In biblical parlance, then, the root image of the church is the *called community* comprised of a mixed multitude of folk. Paul never addressed congregations to whom he wrote as "families," but instead as those "who are called" (Romans 1:6; 1 Corinthians 1:2).

Nevertheless, the popular misconception of the church as family is understandable, especially in settings both liberal and conservative in which prevailing cultural arguments about "family values" have more authority in the church than the Bible does. After all, congregations are "familylike" in a variety of ways. They engage in socialization, acculturation, and norm setting. They are committed to nurturing children. They may eat together, work together, play together, and provide care for their sick and dying together. Marriages within the congregation create literal nuclear and extended families within the larger cohort. Alternatively, congregations often provide surrogate extended families for persons without family as well as for persons without family nearby. Church can become "like family" in many ways.

Furthermore, the widespread use of "family systems theory" or "Bowen theory" in seminary curricula and among pastoral counselors has provided professional reinforcement for this popular but erroneous conception of the church. Popularized by Edwin H. Friedman in his widely influential *Generation to Generation: Family Process in Church and Synagogue* (Guilford Press, 1985), family systems theory frequently elucidates certain aspects of the way churches function (and dysfunction). However, family systems theory inevitably fails when it is pressed into service as a "theory of everything" because a church is a decidedly different kind of organizational system. Family systems theory works—up to a point—not because churches are families, but because churches and families are both social *systems*. The differences between these two systems are considerable and must not be ignored or minimized. For example, in American Protestant churches in particular, persons affiliate with congregations by free and voluntary association, unlike in families where new members are added by being adopted by or born to parents. The fundamental differences in the basic "terms of entry," as well as in the legal and moral authority of the senior members of the system, create relationships between church members and their leaders that are categorically different than those between children and their "father" or "mother." Unlike in families, freely associating persons in most churches may come and go without suffering the psychological or financial consequences of disobeying parental authority. Clearly, certain strategies of parental compulsion may work at home but almost never in the church! The difference is especially evident in those churches in which leaders are chosen by some form of democratic or representative process. When a congregation's membership concludes that the church's leadership is not exhibiting either the character or the quality that is necessary or desired, it has the power to vote the pastoral or lay leadership out, or it may appeal to the bishop for a reassignment of the clergy involved. Would that incompetent or abusive parents could be so summarily dismissed or reassigned! In the end, the obvious organizational and legal complexities of congregations—bound by a "book of order" or "rules of church order," policy manuals, denominational oversight or sanction, state charters, and federal law—invalidate the family theory of the church. Systems theory still applies, but it is *organizational* systems theory rather than family systems theory that pertains most closely to the local congregation and the larger church alike.

To be sure, many congregations continue to operate on a family model by exhibiting attitudes and behaviors similar to those of a traditional Italian family with which I am familiar. If you are born into the family, you are an "in-law," which entitles you on visiting the old home place to sit around the kitchen table where the cigars are plentiful, the wine flows freely, and the conversation is spirited. But if you marry into the family, you are forever an "outlaw," which entitles you to sit primly in the living room sipping what is brought to you from the kitchen as you converse politely with other visiting outlaws, who are welcome in the house but not in the kitchen. A clergywoman more than ten years in her position as an associate pastor concluded a hospital visit with an elderly congregant with prayer and walked to the door. As she did, she overheard the church member comment to a visiting neighbor sitting by her bedside, in a whisper characteristic of Shakespearean actors and the hearing impaired, "She thinks she's one of the ministers at our church." In the house, but not in the kitchen!

In addition to *ekklēsia*, the apostle Paul used another root image for the church: "the body," more specifically "one body in Christ" (Romans 12:5) and "the body of Christ" (1 Corinthians 12:27). It is especially notable that in the passages in which Paul invokes the metaphor of the church as "body," he is explicitly addressing issues of diversity and unity in the church. Romans 12:4-8 reads:

> For as in one body we have many members, and not all the members have the same function, so we, who are many, are one body in Christ, and individually we are members one of another. We have gifts that differ according to the grace given to us: prophecy, in proportion to faith; ministry, in ministering; the teacher, in teaching; the exhorter, in exhortation; the giver, in generosity; the leader, in diligence; the compassionate, in cheerfulness.

As a root metaphor for the church, the "body" with its various members allows Paul to lay claim to both diversity and

unity in the church without compromising the integrity of
either. Paul's longer treatment of the metaphor in 1 Corinthians 12:12-30 (written to a church in which the diversity-in-
unity and unity-in-diversity challenges appear to have been
more immediately pressing than in Rome) includes a repeated insistence on both the independence and the interdependence of the many and the one: "For just as the body
is one and has many members, and all the members of the
body, though many, are one body, so it is with Christ. . . . Indeed, one body does not consist of one member but of many.
. . . Now you are the body of Christ and individually members of it" (vv. 12, 14, 27).

The Christian thinker and apologist C. S. Lewis extended
this root image of the "body" to include "the whole of the
human race" as "one huge organism," an interpretive move
that makes the metaphor no less illuminative of life in the
church:

> Christianity thinks of human individuals not as mere mem-
> bers of a group or items in a list, but as organs in a body—dif-
> ferent from one another and each contributing what no other
> could. When you find yourself wanting to turn your chil-
> dren, or pupils, or even your neighbours, into people exactly
> like yourself, remember that God probably never meant
> them to be like that. You and they are different organs, in-
> tended to do different things. On the other hand, when you
> are tempted not to bother about someone else's troubles be-
> cause they are "no business of yours," remember that though
> he is different from you he is part of the same organism as
> you.[8]

Lewis articulates the diversity-in-unity issue in the context of
the root image of "body."

In addition to "body of Christ," "called community" or
"assembly," and "people of God," there are other possibili-
ties, of course. The book of Acts refers to "the Way" as an expression of "Christian teaching as well as Christians as a
group"[9]: "Meanwhile Saul, still breathing threats and murder

against the disciples of the Lord, went to the high priest and asked him for letters to the synagogues at Damascus, so that if he found any who belonged to *the Way,* men or women, he might bring them bound to Jerusalem" (9:2; see also 19:9, 23; 22:4; 24:14, 22). Paul uses the metaphor of "temple" for the congregation (the pronouns are all plural) when he asks in 1 Corinthians 3:16, "Do you not know that you are *God's temple* and that God's Spirit dwells in you?" (emphasis added). Together, the people are the temple. The congregation of those "called to be saints" is featured as a root image in the salutation to the churches in Corinth and Rome (Romans 1:7; 1 Corinthians 1:2). There are still others. An indispensable question to ask of a congregation's culture is: *What is our root image of the church?* And a second question follows from the first: *Is our root image conducive to cultivating and utilizing "the complex and ever-changing blend of attributes, behaviors, and talents" in our congregation? Or does our root image inhibit it?* Is it not written that the church is a called community, a people of God, a body made up of many diverse individuals, families, and households?

WHY ARE WE HERE?

An often-repeated scenario plays out in a local congregation. A study committee is appointed to address a potentially controversial matter. Its members are selected to ensure that they "represent the diversity in our congregation." Before long, however, it becomes apparent that instead of being an effective working group, the committee is a train wreck. After months of meetings, discussion, debate, argument, hand-wringing, and arm-twisting, the committee finally makes its report to the congregation. Battered by the process, few if any of its members are particularly enthusiastic about the recommendations they make. Shortly after their work is completed, one member of the committee leaves for another church. Two others significantly reduce their level of participation in church life, and two more swear they will "never do that again." The congregation's anxiety level is even higher after the committee's work is done than it was before. If the committee couldn't find "unity in diversity" on this issue, what hope is there for the whole congregation? How could things have gone so wrong?

Short of a miracle occurring, this committee was doomed from the outset because when it was appointed, its mission was reduced, in effect, to demographic representation on the issue it was to study. The individual members of the committee did exactly what they understood themselves to be charged with doing: they each represented a partisan perspective within the congregation, and they championed it to the best of their ability to the bitter end. Had the appointment of the committee been *mission driven* instead of inclusion driven, its members would have been selected based on their ability to listen empathetically to different perspectives, to discuss thoroughly their own assumptions and convictions as well as those of others, and to put the mission and ministry of the congregation ahead of their own and others' particular preferences in their decision making. The committee would have worked to ensure that they heard from and listened to the wide variety of perspectives characteristic of the diversity of the congregation without losing sight of their primary responsibility to arrive at the best possible outcome for the congregation as a whole instead of merely championing its parts. "Mission first" is the mantra of diversity-mature congregations, committees, and leaders in the church. Thomas writes: "The mission is the organization's fundamental purpose. Its mission statement answers the questions: 'Why are we here?' 'What are we endeavoring to do?' "[10]

Among the least compelling potential answers to the questions *Why are we here?* and *What are we endeavoring to do?* is the response "We are here to be diverse" or "We are endeavoring to do diversity." Once again, Lyle Schaller's observation is instructive.

"Our strength is our diversity!" That is an increasingly common slogan among Protestant congregations in the United

States. At least occasionally it is proclaimed as an explanation for the relatively small size of the congregation. When megachurches dominate the religious scene, how does one defend the existence of the congregation averaging eighty-five at worship? One response is to highlight the demographic diversity.[11]

Schaller's statistical analysis that follows reveals how demographically "undiverse" most self-proclaimed "diverse" congregations really are in comparison to the U.S. population at large. For example, in this country, "The median age of those fourteen and over is approximately forty-six years," with a generational breakdown that looks like this: 16 percent are 65 and older; 30 percent are 45-64; 34 percent are 25-44; and 20 percent are 14-24.[12] Few mainline Protestant churches that claim to be diverse succeed in covering the generational spread of the American population at large, with 84 percent of their population fourteen and older being younger than 65. A demographically diverse congregation according to race and nationality would be 70 percent non-Hispanic white; 13 percent black; 12 percent Hispanic; and 4 percent Asian. Where marital status is concerned, the diverse congregation would be made up of one-fourth "single never-married adults age eighteen and over," with an additional one-sixth of the congregation formerly married.[13] The family-makeup data that Schaller cites are nearly a decade old now, but they are still instructive. According to a 1998 survey by the national Opinion Research Center of the University of Chicago, 32 percent of American households were unmarried heterosexual couples without children at home, and 12 percent were unmarried couples with children under the age of fifteen years in the home.[14] Few "diverse" congregations consist of 44 percent unmarried couples!

The common slogan, "Our diversity is our strength," is a reflection of what happens in the church when sociology replaces theology as the dominant mode of discourse and diversity devolves toward idolatry. The faithful theological confession is that "*God* is our . . . strength" (Psalm 46:1, emphasis added), not diversity! Schaller generously and euphemistically accepts this slogan as "highlighting" diversity, when in fact it more often scapegoats it as a reason for the small size and struggling character of a local congregation. But the extraordinary racial, ethnic, generational, and socioeconomic diversity of many rapidly growing Pentecostal or charismatic churches around the country reveals that demographic diversity is no impediment to vitality or growth in the church. Instead, it is the loss of clarity and conviction about mission and identity that destroys vitality and growth.

Different local congregations articulate their mission quite variously—when they articulate it at all. Indeed, one of the greatest difficulties congregational leaders face in addressing diversity in the church is a congregational lack of clarity about mission. Until a congregation adequately identifies and articulates its mission to itself, many of its congregants (and clergy as well) will assume that it is the church's mission to "take a stand" (consistent with their own, of course) on certain (but not other) hot-button topics in the current culture wars. But leaping from stand to stand like a sifaka lemur only politicizes and trivializes the church by reducing it to one more political or social special-interest group and destines it eventually to endangered-species status. William Cavanaugh points out the fallacy of the special-interest church by appealing to the Greek origin of the root image of the *ekklēsia*, "the assembly." In the Greek city-state, "*ekklēsia* meant the assembly of all those with citizen rights in a given city. The early Christians thus refused the available language of guild or association (such as *koinon, collegium*) and asserted that *the church was not gathered around particular interests, but was interested in all things*; it was an assembly of the whole."[15] Once again, Verene's eloquence, "speaking of the whole" rather than only of the part comes into view.[16] Without clear, compelling, and widely communicated answers to the mission-first questions *Why are we here?* and *What are we endeavoring to do?* churches are at the mercy of their congregants' and clergys' whims and prevailing cultural winds.

The Gospels depict Jesus as making decisions based on his mission, as in Luke 4:42-44, when he resists the efforts of the crowd to keep him where he is: "The crowds were looking for him; and when they reached him, they wanted to prevent him from leaving them. But he said to them, 'I must proclaim the good news of the kingdom of God to the other cities also; for I was sent for this purpose.' So he continued proclaiming the message in the synagogues of Judea." Clearly, the shifting tide of public opinion was not Jesus' criterion for determining the locus and the content of his ministry. His clarity about his mission and the depth of his commitment to it brought him into conflict not only with the religious and political authorities of his day but with his own followers as well, as in his first prediction of his death in Mark 8:31-33:

> Then he began to teach them that the Son of Man must undergo great suffering, and be rejected by the elders, the chief priests, and the scribes, and be killed, and after three days rise again. He said all this quite openly. And Peter took him aside and began to rebuke him. But turning and looking at his disciples, he rebuked Peter and said, "Get behind me, Satan! For you are setting your mind not on divine things but on human things."

In other passages, the New Testament reports that Jesus periodically had to remind his followers to focus on mission instead of their own special interests and inclinations. For example, in Acts 1, the Risen Lord redirects the attention of the apostles from speculation about the end time when they ask, "Lord, is this the time when you will restore the kingdom to Israel?" (v. 6). Jesus' response calls them to focus on their *mission as witnesses* instead of their speculative interests: "It is not for you to know the times or periods that the Father has set by his own authority. But you will receive power when the Holy Spirit has come upon you; and *you will be my witnesses* in Jerusalem, in all Judea and Samaria, and to the ends of the earth" (vv. 7-8). Luke's account of the mission of the twelve has honed it down to a mission-centered focus:

> Then Jesus called the twelve together and gave them power and authority over all demons and to cure diseases, and he sent them out *to proclaim the kingdom of God and to heal.* He said to them, "Take nothing for your journey, no staff, nor bag, nor bread, nor money—not even an extra tunic. Whatever house you enter, stay there, and leave from there. Wherever they do not welcome you, as you are leaving that town shake the dust off your feet as a testimony against them." They departed and went through the villages, *bringing the good news and curing diseases* everywhere. (Luke 9:1-6, emphasis added)

A similarly extreme mission-focused set of instructions is given to the seventy, including "greet no one on the road" (10:4), as they are to "cure the sick who are there, and say to them, 'The kingdom of God has come near to you'" (v. 9). In both passages, Jesus' followers are instructed to allow nothing to distract them from the mission on which they have been "sent" (9:2; 10:1). As in Luke and Acts, mission—"commission," as it is usually referred to—is the focus of Jesus' famous last words in Matthew's Gospel: "Go therefore and make disciples of all nations, baptizing them in the name of the Father and of the Son and of the Holy Spirit, and teaching them to obey everything that I have commanded you" (Matthew 28:19-20).

As Jesus models it, there is no substitute for clarity of mission and commitment to it. By focusing on *mission first* and diversity second, diversity is correctly identified as a *means for mission* rather than confusing it with the mission itself or scapegoating it as an impediment to mission: *How can we best utilize our diversity to fulfill our mission?* Not surprisingly, then, where there is no clarity of mission, there is no compelling motive for nurturing diversity. For congregational cultures mired in either an affirmative-action or an inclusion mode, "diversity is limited to making things right with minorities and women," as Thomas puts it; in other words, mere demographic representation.[17] But in organizations characterized by Thomas as exhibiting a higher degree of "diversity maturity," the motive is entirely different. For them, the compelling motive for cultivating their diversity is enhancing their ability to fulfill their mission. Thomas calls this rationale "the compelling business motive."[18] In the church, it is *the compelling mission-and-ministry motive*. The only compelling motive for cultivating diversity in the church is to enhance and expand the church's ability to fulfill its mission. To operate on the basis of any other motive is to confuse a given with a goal and to mistake a means for an end. To those congregations who say, "Our diversity is our strength," the mission-focused response is, "Then tell us the ways you are capitalizing on your diversity to carry out your mission and ministry." Very few of them can. In the current American context, diversity is merely a given. However, *how effectively a congregation utilizes its diversity*—"the complex and ever-changing blend of attributes, behaviors, and talents" of the people who are among its number—*is a mission-critical capability* and an indispensable means toward the church's end of fulfilling its mission.

WHAT IS REQUIRED?

One of the most valuable aspects of Thomas's framework for dealing with diversity is the distinction he makes between "a *genuine requirement* and a preference, convenience, or tradition."[19] Thomas writes:

> Often a decision to accept or reject a certain element of a diversity mixture is rationalized with, "This is something we need," when in fact the truth is closer to, "I like it better this way," or "I don't agree with this behavior." Effective diversity respondents can identify the genuine requirements and consistently use them as a basis for making decisions about diversity.[20]

As challenging as this distinction is in business settings, it is even more difficult in churches for whom "tradition" is often a core theological ingredient in their identity. In place of Thomas's "tradition," it might be more helpful in congregational settings to say "traditional practices," as in "how we've always done it." Thomas's distinction between the required and the merely customary, preferred or traditional practice is eminently biblical.

One of the most familiar and best-loved verses in the Old Testament prophets is Micah 6:8: "*What does the* LORD *require of you* but to do justice, and to love kindness, and to walk humbly with your God?" (emphasis added). This clarifying question is itself a response to a series of inquiries from a would-be worshiper about divine preferences: "Wherewith shall I come before the LORD, and bow myself before the high God? shall I come . . . with burnt offerings, with calves of a year old? Will the LORD be pleased with thousands of rams, or with ten thousands of rivers of oil? Shall I give my firstborn for my transgression, the fruit of my body for the sin of my soul?" (Micah 6:6-7 KJV). The prophet's response to these questions draws on (or perhaps creates) a distinction between the covenantal practice of sacrifices and offerings and the covenantal *requirement* "to do justice, and to love kindness, and to walk humbly with your God." Similarly, in Mark 12:28, the Jewish scribe who inquired of Jesus concerning "which commandment is the first of all" responds to Jesus' answer with the assertion, "You are right, Teacher; you have truly said that 'he is one, and besides him there is no other'; and 'to love him with all the heart, and with all the understanding, and with all the strength,' and 'to love one's neighbor as oneself,'—*this is much more important than* all whole burnt offerings and sacrifices" (Mark 12:32-33, emphasis added). Jesus goes on to affirm the scribe's distinction between what is desirable and what is required: "When Jesus saw that he answered wisely, he said to him, 'You are not far from the kingdom of God'" (v. 34). The capacity of a congregation to make such distinctions between what is required and what is preferred, convenient or merely traditional is a key aspect of congregational culture in dealing with diversity.

A man in his mid-twenties, recently married to a woman who had grown up in the church they were attending, was accosted after worship by a diminutive woman in her eighties, more than sixty years a member of the congregation. "You should be ashamed to come to church dressed that way!" she announced as she looked with disdain at his polo shirt, khaki slacks, and loafers. Not surprisingly, this diversity tension over Sunday-morning fashion quickly became a topic of conversation in the young couple's Sunday school class—and in the wife's mother's class as well. The young man's mother-in-law was incensed, as she was quite pleased that her son-in-law was attending the church with her daughter. What he wore was inconsequential to her. The husband and wife approached their pastor for counsel. "We don't have a dress code here," the pastor said. "What you have been wearing is fine. Let me see what I can do to help clarify things for all of us." Discussion with the congregation's lay leadership at its next monthly meeting resulted in wide agreement that although the congregation's worship was fairly formal and most people preferred to "dress up" for it, younger individuals and families in particular seemed to prefer less dressy attire. Several longtime lay leaders volunteered to begin wearing more casual clothing periodically as an indication of their solidarity with younger people in the congregation who "dressed down." Conversation with the church staff followed. The activities ministry planned a Sunday afternoon "May Day Play Day" for young families on the church's ball fields. That Sunday morning was declared a "dress-down Sunday" in conjunction with the event. On another Sunday, the several dozen participants in an afternoon citywide "walk for the homeless" were encouraged to wear their event T-shirts to Sunday school and worship that morning, and the welcome pointed out to the congregation that they could identify the participants by their dress. Later in the fall, when the congregation celebrated its commitments to its capital campaign with a Sunday-morning churchwide breakfast before worship, the invitations to the event noted, "Casual dress optional."

Finally, one Sunday in the course of a sermon, the pastor talked about the theological symbolism of dressing for worship. The sermon explained why worship leaders in that congregation wear robes and stoles instead of business attire or a tuxedo and tails or a black cocktail dress or shorts and a T-shirt. The sermon described how important the tradition of wearing their "Sunday finest" is to people who use "dressing up for church" to help them signify that worship is sacred time set apart from the ordinary and mundane affairs of their daily existence. But the sermon also pointed out that there are some women and men for whom attending church in their weekday business attire feels like worshiping in their "work clothes"—precisely what some in the "dress-up" crowd are trying to avoid! "The only place I wear a dress and pantyhose is at work," a woman says. "I come to worship God on my own time, not my company's time. If I wear what I wear to work, it doesn't feel like church to me." For some men, the tie they wear during the week is a noose around their necks, a sign and symbol of the strangling power of a job they despise. To feel close to God in worship, these women and men must loosen up, dress down, "come as they are" to worship God instead of costumed in the power clothing or required uniform of their workplace. "There is no dress requirement for worship in this congregation," the pastor said. "We don't require people to 'dress up,' and we don't require people to 'dress down.' Instead, we expect people to dress in the way that best prepares them to be open to encountering the presence of God in worship." Distinguishing between what is required and what is a preference, convenience, or traditional practice is a key component in effective diversity leadership.

The process is worth noting. A point of diversity tension arose between two congregants. The issue on which the conflict arose had implications for the wider congregation, so instead of being ignored (or suppressed) the matter became a topic of both informal and formal conversation in a variety of congregational venues. In the course of the conversations, the diversity issue was not framed as a conflict between "the main" (the older and dressed up) and "the other" (the younger and dressed down). Instead, it was taken up as identifying a theologically oriented difference within the total collective mixture that had resulted in tension between some. Conversation led to clarification, and clarification led to action involving "the total collective mixture." It would be a mistake to conclude that the result was a collective relativism—anything goes—or an attempt to be all things to all people. Neither was the case. First, in the course of making a previously implicit diversity tension explicit and then dealing with it forthrightly, the congregation's staff and lay leadership came to a twofold conclusion: a variety of dress was accepted and supported, and this congregation's "requirement" regarding clothing was a willingness on the part of those who dressed up *and* on the part of those who dressed down *to bear with one another and to build one another up*. There would no doubt be "casualists" who when they saw the business attire of others would conclude that they could not be comfortable worshiping in this congregation: "casual only" was what they required for worship, and this congregation would not meet their dress requirements. There would also be "formalists" who would see some people wearing casual clothes and conclude that this was too "low" a church for them: "dress up only" was what they required, and this congregation would not meet their dress requirements. *Accepting and supporting both* modes of dress was identified as the congregation's requirement. Second, anything did not go. The limits of casual were clarified one Sunday morning when a young soloist wore a cropped top and below-the-hip jeans. Some in attendance were scandalized, others were energized; some were merely amused, while still others appear to have slept through it. "I have nothing against tummies and navels," the pastor said to the minister of worship and music after the service. "But she should probably wear a choir robe the next time she sings if she dresses that way." The minister of worship and music talked with the young woman about appropriate attire (whether casual or dressy) for people in leadership roles, and she chose to dress more conservatively the next time she sang rather than wear a robe. On matters large or small, the progression from conflict to conversation to clarification to action is a model for distinguishing effectively between the requirements and the preferences, conveniences or traditional practices that contribute to a congregation's culture. However, where there is no clarity of mission, there can be no adequate basis for distinguishing between requirements and preferences, conveniences or traditional practices. Indeed, where there is no clarity of mission, there is only preference, convenience, and traditional practice, a familiar and deadly condition in many congregations.

Effective diversity leadership in the church addresses congregational culture with the three questions: *What is our root image of the church? What is our mission?* and *What do we require?*

THE MISSION-FIRST
JESUS

A Sermon on John 8:31-59

I t is as ugly and divisive an exchange as any you will find
in Scripture, this conversation between Jesus and a group
of his followers who are identified in John 8:31 as "the
Jews who had believed in him." Dialogue disintegrates into
diatribe. Death threats and demonization take center stage.
And as if the war of words in the text were not bad enough,
the combustible content of this conversation has been mined
for centuries to fuel animosity and even violence on the part
of some Christians toward individual Jews, Jewish communities, and the vibrant and living faith that is Judaism.

Across three decades of preaching and teaching, I have
found this passage so offensive that I have always passed by
it quickly—and on the other side of the interpretive street, as
it were. Simply put, the Jesus portrayed in John 8:31-59 is
not a Jesus I want to see or follow. The Jesus I want to see in
the Gospels and follow is the one who says, "Father, forgive
them; for they do not know what they are doing" (Luke
23:34), not a Jesus who says, "You are from your father the
devil" (John 8:44). I want to see and follow the Jesus who
says, "Blessed are the peacemakers, for they will be called
children of God" (Matthew 5:9), not a Jesus who says, "Do
not think that I have come to bring peace to the earth; I have
not come to bring peace, but a sword" that will divide families—and with them communities (Matthew 10:34). Simply
put, John 8:31-59 assails my most treasured assumptions

about Jesus, and it forces me to reckon with a Jesus in the Gospels who is someone other than a mascot of my own design and liking, someone other than a champion of my own preferences and persuasions.

The passage begins innocuously enough in verse 31. In a manner of speaking characteristic of the Gospel of John, Jesus says, "If you continue in my word, you are truly my disciples." A now beloved line about truth and freedom follows that benign admonition: "You will know the truth, and the truth will make you free." Taken at face value, these words would not appear to be contentious or controversial. But in the setting in which they are spoken, the followers to whom Jesus speaks quickly take issue with them.

The setting in which Jesus speaks these words is rife with conflict and controversy. Taken together, chapters 7 and 8 in John's Gospel are a masterfully narrated depiction of chaos and confusion. At the beginning of chapter 7, we are told that religious and political authorities—who are referred to as "the Jews" in John's Gospel—"were looking for an opportunity to kill him" (7:1). All the way through chapter 7, the crowds are presented as divided in their opinions of Jesus, as though they were shouting back and forth at one another in antiphonal fashion (7:12, 25, 31, 32, 40-43). The temple police, the chief priests, and the Pharisees exchange furious accusations among themselves (vv. 45-48). They denounce the crowds as ignorant and accursed (v. 49), and they debate the propriety of a judgment against Jesus without a hearing (vv. 50-52). And all the while, running beneath the surface of the public turmoil are chilling currents of discord and conflict within Jesus' own circle. Late in chapter 6 we are told that many among his followers found his teaching "too difficult," and "because of this many of his disciples turned back and no longer went about with him" (6:66). At the same time, it is revealed that one of his own will betray him (6:64, 70-71). The abandonment and betrayal is brought even closer to home when it is reported, "not even his brothers believed in him" (7:5). In fact, Jesus himself is portrayed as not being of a single mind. In 7:6-8 he tells his brothers to go on to Jerusalem without him because he is not going to the festival, but two verses later he ends up going after all (7:10)!

The passage in front of us, John 8:31-59, is the high watermark of the chaos and confusion in chapters 7 and 8. The situation is so fluid that it is not even entirely clear who Jesus' conversation partners are at various points in the passage. For example, in verses 31-36, it is clear enough that Jesus is addressing people who have "believed" in him. But his words in verses 42-47 sound as though they are aimed at persons who have rejected him all along.[1] Although some commentators have suggested that the text has been mangled by dislocation and fragmentation, the ambiguity and incongruity of the discourse as it stands are quite compelling. In the dynamic fluidity of controversy and conflict, it is sometimes impossible to discern whether conversation partners are friends or foes. And as every leader knows from experience, in times of conflict and high anxiety, statements intended for one audience are all too often appropriated by or applied to another without regard for the speaker's intent!

So when Jesus is portrayed as addressing a group identified as some among the Jewish authorities "who had believed in him," he speaks in a conflict-riddled setting of public turmoil and private discord shot through with disagreements, accusations, complaints, and contrary-to-fact statements. Not surprisingly, then, what Jesus says about "word," "discipleship," "truth," and "freedom" in verses 31-32 is subjected to immediate scrutiny. To be sure, the simple question asked of a teacher by students, "What do you mean?" lies at the heart of the teaching and learning enterprise. Furthermore, although "word," "discipleship," and "truth" are already familiar themes in the Gospel of John, "freedom" is a note that is sounded for the very first time. The audience in the text is surely justified in asking, "What do you mean by saying, 'You will be made free'?" But in this case, when the students ask their question, they reveal not openness to learning but resistance to hearing by putting forward two self-serving assertions that challenge what they presume to be the assumptions behind what Jesus has said: "We . . . have never been slaves to anyone," they say, and "We are descendants of Abraham." No savvy teacher would fail to recognize in their response a greater concern for self-justification than for understanding, and the verbal battle is joined.

In a succession of accusations, insinuations, and insults, Jesus and his audience become thoroughly alienated from each other. In the CliffsNotes version, as it were, the tiff goes like this:

Jesus: You are slaves—to sin. You are trying to kill me, and that means that the word I have brought from the Father is not in you.

Audience: Abraham is our father.

Jesus: You are trying to kill me, and that makes you children of some unknown father.

Audience: God is our father.

Jesus: The devil is your father. I'm telling the truth, and you don't hear it because you are not from God.

Audience: You have a demon, not us.

Jesus: Not me, my word saves from death.

Audience: You must have a demon! Avoid death? Who do you claim to be?

Jesus: God whom you claim as your father glorifies me, and Abraham whom you claim as your father rejoiced to see my day.

Audience: You are too young to have seen Abraham!

Jesus: Before Abraham was, I am.

After that stunning claim to transcend time and space, the conversation and the chapter close with Jesus' audience picking up stones, evidently to stone him for blasphemy, but he hides from them and makes his way out of the temple precinct.

So who is this Jesus of John 8? We certainly would not recognize him as the one of whom the Ethiopian eunuch was reading in Acts 8:32-35: "Like a sheep he was led to the slaughter, and like a lamb silent before its shearer, so he does not open his mouth" (see Isaiah 53:7). John 8 depicts a verbally combative Jesus who baits and bashes his audience. If they weren't ready to kill him when he started speaking in John 8:31, the fact that they are ready to do so at the end of the chapter is nothing short of a self-fulfilling prophecy. This Jesus splashes oil on a fire that was already threatening to consume him.

Contrary to centuries of Christian misappropriation of the vitriolic discourse in John 8, the Jesus of this chapter is no "victim" of a "conspiracy"—Jewish or otherwise—against him. Instead, he is clearly an active agent in his own demise. This Jesus goes to great pains to alienate his supporters and infuriate his opponents. When some of his disciples complain about how difficult his teaching is, his response to them is so insensitive to their concerns that they are sufficiently alienated to abandon him (6:60-66). This Jesus acknowledges his own responsibility for calling his betrayer among the twelve (6:70). This Jesus chooses to go to the festival in Jerusalem in spite of his own better judgment to remain in Galilee (7:8-10). Knowing full well that the authorities are after him on account of the uproar his ministry has created (7:1), this Jesus still cannot bring himself to participate in the festival "in secret" as he had originally intended when he went (7:10). Instead, he elects to teach publicly—and in the temple precinct, no less (7:14). And when he does, he opts to engage in an accusatory and inflammatory exchange with his listeners (7:16-24). Finally, in chapter 8, in a conversation with a cohort of his followers well connected to the authorities ("the Jews"), he pursues a line of discourse that inflames their fury instead of cultivating their favor as friends who could do for him what the prophet

Jeremiah's well-placed supporters were able to do repeatedly—keep him alive in spite of his offensive preaching, even in the temple precinct. Clearly, the Jesus of John 8 is on a mission that will end in his death, and he will not be turned back from it. In fact, he will speak and act at every turn to assure that his mission is accomplished. It is Jesus' active agency, not a "Jewish conspiracy," that is the primary driver in the turmoil and discord, conflict and controversy that eventually lead to his crucifixion. Even in this most inflammatory chapter in what some have called the most "anti-Jewish" Gospel in the New Testament, the character of Jesus—not the character of his supporters or his opponents—is embarrassingly and courageously responsible for the deadly journey that he is on.

If this Jesus is no mascot for the "culture of blame" for his death that has become so much a part of the history of Christian preaching and teaching of this text, then neither is he a mascot for the more recent variations on this culture inside the church: the culture of victimization and the culture of the persecuted minority. The Jesus of John 8 is neither a model victim nor a persecuted representative of a minority. This Jesus is an active agent who faces the consequences of his own activism willingly and courageously. This Jesus does not represent the culture that has become a society of last resort for those of us in ministry and in leadership in the church who feel beaten up and beaten down in our calling. We appeal to our treasured assumption of a persecuted and victimized Jesus, despised and rejected through no fault of his own, to justify our unwillingness to take responsibility for our own complicity in our failures in ministry and the pain in leadership that we are experiencing. The behavior of Jesus in John 7–8 is reminiscent of one of my favorite book titles ever: *Why Is It That Every Time I Get Stabbed in the Back, My Fingerprints Are on the Knife?* by Jerry Harvey. This Jesus is an embarrassingly active agent in his own demise, as are we all, and the behavior he models is not victimization but a courageous accountability prepared to accept at every turn the consequences of his words and actions.

Nor is the Jesus of John 8 a mascot for the perennially popular cult of institutional self-preservation. Current mantras of this cult include, "Can't we all just get along?" and "Let's get everyone together and talk this out," as though talk were a panacea for every ill. John 8:31-59 calls into question the efficacy of these familiar cries in the church. In some circles of the church, "diversity" is the rallying cry for institutional self-preservation. Chapters 6 through 8 of John's Gospel indicate that Jesus' teaching attracted a fascinatingly diverse constituency: rural Galileans, urbane Jerusalemites, at least some from among the religious and political authorities, the common rabble of the festival crowd, and at one point even some among the temple police. The opportunity was ripe for Jesus to model what is called in our time "diversity management" to consolidate and institutionalize a movement that would produce in this world a diversely populated kingdom. Surely the future was bright for this Jesus to be canonized as the patron saint of diversity. But at every turn, instead of acting and speaking in a fashion that would build on his success to consolidate and institutionalize a diverse constituency, his willfully divisive rhetoric and behavior indicate that his commitment to his mission trumped self-preservation and institution building. Blessing the ties that bind appears to be the farthest thing from this Jesus' mind.

I, for one, have intentionally ignored John 8:31-59, both because of what it says and how it has been used, and not in the least because I see in it a Jesus whom I would still cross the street to avoid, if I were given the chance. And yet, the Jesus of John 8 is one whom I—and all of us together—ignore to the detriment of our respective callings in ministry and our responsibilities for leadership. In the conflict and controversy, the turmoil and discord to which we are called as leaders in the church, nothing less will do than active agency, courageous accountability, and an unflagging commitment to "mission first." Nothing less will do

CHAPTER 6

DIVERSITY LEADERSHIP: QUESTIONS OF THE INDIVIDUAL JOURNEY

As R. Roosevelt Thomas Jr. has observed, "Diversity efforts often succeed or fail based on the impact of the organization's culture."[1] Still, the role and the responsibility of the individuals who lead an organization can hardly be overstated when it comes to the character and quality—and change—of the organization's culture. Thomas writes:

> We expect the leaders of our organizations to lead: to define the . . . mission and vision, articulate it with passion to inspire everyone else, create strategies to enact the vision . . . and shape the underlying climate within which all these elements come together as people go about the day-to-day doing of their job.[2]

Clearly, then, cultivating wise and effective diversity leadership in the church requires asking questions of individuals as well as of congregational culture. By asking questions of ourselves, we can embark on what Thomas calls "the individual journey" of cultivating "diversity maturity" or diversity expertise.[3] Among the indispensable steps on this journey, Thomas identifies these six: examining one's own attitudes, acknowledging one's own role, monitoring one's own behavior, increasing opportunities to learn, putting diversity leadership into practice whenever possible, and reviewing priorities and devising a plan.[4]

WHERE ARE YOU?

The first question asked of human beings in the Bible is the divine inquiry, "Where are you?" (Genesis 3:9). On the face of it, it is a curious question. After all, if God doesn't know, who does? The rabbinic tradition has long held that the point of this query was to engage the man and the woman in conversation that would provide an opportunity for self-examination and confession.[5] *Examining one's own attitudes*, then, is a crucial first step on the individual journey.[6]

The leading question is: *In the presence of persons with what attributes, perceptions, attitudes, or behaviors does my "diversity response mechanism" kick in? And when it does, what is my first response to that diversity? Conquest? Coexistence? Coercion? Conversion? Compassionate action? Conversation? Collaboration?* We all have a primary response—the one most typical of us under ordinary circumstances. In settings outside the ordinary or on peculiar issues we may find ourselves responding differently than our typical response. Under stress, we may respond differently yet again. The essential insight in *examining my own attitudes* is that *we are all "diversity challenged."* None of us has entirely "clean hands and pure hearts" (Psalm 24:4). If we claim to, "we deceive ourselves, and the truth is not in us" (1 John 1:8).

It is a particularly hard lesson for some liberals to learn that they are every bit as "diversity challenged" as conservatives. Liberals are rightly critical of many conservatives who will broach no dissent from their treasured theological, political, and social assumptions and arguments. But what many liberals in churches fail to recognize about themselves is that they can be every bit as dogmatic and "exclusive" as many conservatives on selected diversity issues. For example, some liberals in churches pride themselves on "welcoming and affirming" gay, lesbian, bisexual, and transgendered persons, while at the same time routinely condemning and vilifying people in the church whom they caricature as "homophobes." In some circles, "homophobes" are the new "homosexuals," neither welcomed nor affirmed. The dismissive attitudes on the left and on the right are identical: only the persons treated with contempt differ. Thomas's distinction between a commitment to "inclusion" and a commitment to diversity is extremely valuable on this point.[7] "Inclusion" identifies particular populations as "others" who are the target of the church's welcome and affirmation. Those who do not fit the category to be "included" (or who do not support the effort) are fair game for disdain, derision, and perhaps even exclusion. Diversity, however, insists that all are welcome, not just some who are singled out for welcome and affirmation. For conservatives and liberals alike, self-critical reflection on our own attitudes is an essential first step to increase our wisdom and effectiveness in diversity leadership.

Another way to ask the question of self-examination is, *What attributes, perceptions, attitudes, or behaviors give me the most difficulty in accepting, working with, or learning from people who exhibit them?* That question can help each of us identify the locus of our own "diversity challenge."

A consultant surprised a male senior pastor during a coaching session when he suggested that the reason that the pastor was having difficulty relating to a staff colleague was because "she thinks like a woman." The pastor was immediately offended by what struck him as an allegation that he was a chauvinist.

"Wait a minute," he objected. "I get along great with two other staff colleagues who are women."

"Yes, you do," said the consultant. "They are veterans of church staffs. They both think like men to survive in a man's world."

"That sounds like gender bias to me!" the pastor retorted.

"Maybe it does," the consultant responded, "but what you have described to me is your difficulty in working with a person who doesn't think linearly, who leads with emotion, and who has a tendency to freeze or to flee rather than fight. Call it what you will. *You have a problem* because her processing style is different from yours."

Differences in thinking or processing style are a frequent cause of diversity tension in church staffs, committees, and congregations. The consultant's challenge to the pastor to examine his own attitudes altered the question the pastor was asking from "What is wrong with this staff member?" to *"What must I do* to understand, work effectively with, *and benefit from* the perspective that this person's mode of thinking brings to our staff and church?" That is a wiser and more effective individual response to diversity than asking, "Why doesn't she 'get it'?" or "What's 'wrong' with him?"

WHAT IS THIS THAT YOU HAVE DONE?

"What is this that you have done?" is the question asked of the woman in the garden in Genesis 3:13, after the man failed to take responsibility for his own actions and chose instead to blame his sin on the woman and on God when he replied, "The woman whom you gave to be with me, she gave me the fruit from the tree" (v. 12). This divine inquiry accentuates two more steps on the individual journey: *acknowledging one's own role* and *monitoring one's own behavior.* If, as Thomas defines it, diversity is "any significant collective mixture that includes similarities as well as differences," then *everyone in the congregation plays a role in the diversity.* In the apostle Paul's image in 1 Corinthians 12:12-27, we are all the various members and organs of the body. Every one of us exhibits aspects of the congregation's diversity: generation, gender, ethnicity, faith development, spiritual type, religious experience, denominational origin, congregational connectedness, personality type, family dynamics, attitude, perspective, and behavior. That being the case, it is impossible for any of us to avoid the question, *What is my role in the "complex and ever-changing blend of attributes, behaviors, and talents that make up the 'total collective mixture' " of the congregation of which I am a part?*[8] Each of us constitutes the diversity in the body.

Acknowledging our own role can be especially difficult for two sets of people in local congregations. One set is made up of individuals who think of themselves (consciously or unconsciously) as part of "the main" group whose assumptions and expectations are being challenged or threatened by "others" whom "the main" consider to be "the diversity" in the congregation. The "main" might be determined by generation or by gender, by denominational origin or by ethnicity. The "main" could also cut across other lines of difference to coincide, for example, with the cohort of members who joined the congregation during the long tenure of a dearly loved and respected former pastor. This "main" group is now confronted not only with the difficulty of adapting to a new pastor but also to a cohort of eager newcomers whose loyalties are to the current leadership they know rather than to the former leadership they never knew. In this scenario, as in many others, it is an enormous challenge for individuals who consider themselves part of "the main" to acknowledge their own role as "the diversity" in the church.

Another set of people for whom acknowledging their own role is particularly difficult are those persons whose primary response to diversity is either "coexistence" or "collaboration." These individuals frequently fail to understand that their comfort level with certain attributes, attitudes, or behaviors can actually *exacerbate* diversity tension in a congregation. "I don't have a problem with it" (whatever "it" may happen to be), says one of these individuals. "How can you *not* have a problem with it?" another member asks incredulously. "You *have* to have a problem with it. *Everybody* has a problem with it!" Now, instead of merely being dyadic—between persons exhibiting "it" and persons who have a problem with "it"—the diversity tension has opened on an additional front between those who have a problem with "it" and those who don't, entirely apart from those who exhibit "it"! This tendency toward triangulation is why diversity tension can ratchet up suddenly when an initial tension over one aspect of diversity unexpectedly morphs into heated, systemwide conflict as various individuals or groups defend their own responses to "it" over against other responses. Thus, a curious feature of diversity leadership within the total collective mixture is that it is not like surgery in which a physician stands outside a patient and operates. Instead, diversity leadership is an operation on a body that includes the physician as one of its vital organs. This incongruous image captures the complexity of effective diversity leadership, which requires leaders' self-critical acknowledgment of their own multifaceted role in the body as both patient and physician. "Physician, heal thyself," indeed (Luke 4:23 KJV).

In *monitoring my own behavior*, a key component in effective diversity leadership is the capacity for listening and taking counsel. There is a widespread tendency among leaders in churches to surround themselves with like-minded associates. A long-standing practice among pastors is the cultivation of a "pastor's party" who becomes the pastor's primary circle of communication, counsel, and support. When it comes to diversity leadership, such a party can be invaluable or insidious—and sometimes simultaneously so. In monitoring my own behavior, an important question is: *To whom do I listen, and why?*

A new senior pastor walked into the office of the church's longtime minister of administration for the first time. His eyes fell on a small plaque declaring in Myers-Briggs lingo, "ISTJ spoken here." He nearly laughed out loud as he thought to himself, "This is a match made in heaven . . . or we are going to drive each other nuts!" In Myers-Briggs terminology, the pastor was an ENFP, an "opposite" on each point of the scale. Seeing the differences, he anticipated immediately that this staff member would become either a source of constant conflict in perception, attitude, and expectations or an invaluable sounding board and coleader, because she would always think about and respond to things from a very different perspective than his own. Indeed, both of the pastor's first impressions eventually proved true: it was a match made in heaven, even when they drove each other nuts. It is a clear warning sign for the health of diversity leadership when we find ourselves gravitating toward the company of those who are most like us and who think most like us. Asking ourselves the question about our own behavior, *Whose counsel am I seeking out as I attempt to lead?* can help us identify whether we are tilting toward homogeneity of perspective or authentically embracing the invaluable diversity of our congregation and staff.

WHY COULD WE NOT CAST IT OUT?

Jesus' disciples ask this question in Mark 9:28, after they were unable to exorcise an unclean spirit from a child who was possessed. The disciples had succeeded in exorcisms previously, according to Mark 6:13, which reports: "They cast out many demons, and anointed with oil many who were sick and cured them." When his followers were surprised at their own failure, Jesus responded, "This kind can come out only through prayer" (9:29). Jesus' *post mortem* on the disciples' failure indicates that previous capability and prior experience are not always enough. New challenges constantly present themselves and necessitate *increasing opportunities to learn.*

In addition to the many workshops, conferences, books, and articles that are available to leaders, opportunities to learn can be as simple as *asking instead of assuming.* Leaders in churches, especially pastors and staff members, have a tendency to assume that we understand the perceptions, attitudes, and behaviors of the individuals with whom we are working or to whom we are ministering. Once we succeed in "connecting the dots" in a pattern that makes sense to us, we move on in the assumption that we understand that person. Ironically, in our assumption of our own omniscience we fail to emulate God, who in Genesis 3 invited the man and the woman in the garden to speak for themselves by suspending judgment long enough to ask the question that invited self-examination and confession: "Where are you?" More often than we want to admit, all of us relate to certain people in our churches on the basis of conscious or unconscious assumptions related to attributes such as age, race, gender, education, political affiliation, and so on. But as Thomas points out, "There is as much attitudinal, perceptual, and behavioral diversity within demographic groups as among them."[9]

Martin Luther King Jr.'s famous line about Sunday morning at 11:00 being the most segregated hour in America can be instructive on this point. Racial homogeneity in American churches remains a public and visible vestige of the American commonwealth's original sin, slavery, even if it also reflects cultural and theological differences that have taken on a life of their own apart from their origins in the eras of American racial oppression and apartheid. However, homogeneity of attributes by no means signifies a dearth of diversity in perspective, attitude, and behavior. For example, for a short time in the 1960s, the lay leadership of the congregation I serve posted deacons at the front doors to the sanctuary on Sunday mornings to turn away any "troublemakers" (read: black persons) who might attempt to attend worship. Simultaneously, however, other lay leaders in the congregation were among the larger community's most ardent activists and leaders who were working assiduously and successfully to integrate the public school system, places of business, and all walks of life in town, including churches. A respected member of a men's Sunday school class, J. Martin England, made several trips to Atlanta to meet with Dr. King to assist in setting up an annuity that would help provide for his family in the event that anything happened to him. Only a woefully unsophisticated or willfully ignorant analysis would conclude that the attributes "white and southern" meant that there was uniformity in perspective, attitude, and behavior among the worshipers. Thomas's observation bears repeating: "There is as much attitudinal, perceptual, and behavioral diversity within demographic groups as among them."

"I need to talk with you about Sunday's sermon," she said, getting right to the point as she sat down in her pastor's office. Her pastor wasn't surprised. She knew that this woman and her husband were among the congregation's more conservative members, both theologically and politically. In her sermon on Sunday, the pastor had proclaimed that extending the love of God in Jesus Christ meant welcoming and treating as equals before God persons of every description: rich and poor, old and young, black and white, heterosexual and homosexual.

"I understand," the pastor said. "I have heard that a number of people are unhappy with what I said."

"Actually, I'm here to thank you for what you said," she responded firmly. "My husband and I have gone through a terrible time recently, ever since our best friend's daughter, who has been like our own daughter to us, told her mother that she is a lesbian. We prayed about it, and we lay awake at night crying over it. Last week we finally decided that we have known her and loved her since she was an infant, and we are not going to stop loving her now. Thank you for including her in your sermon and for including her in the love of God."

"I had no idea you were going through that," the pastor said quietly. "How can I help you now that I know?"

In addition to illustrating our failure to anticipate the breadth of diversity in perspectives and attitudes that can exist within a narrowly defined demographic group, this conversation also points to the error of assuming that just because we know where someone *was at one time*, therefore we know where she or he *is now*. Perceptions change. Attitudes adjust. Behavior adapts. Adaptation and change characterize the individual life story of the majority of people who make up "the complex and *ever-changing* blend of attributes, behaviors, and talents" in a local congregation. Asking instead of assuming is a daily opportunity for continuing education in diversity leadership.

WHO WILL TRUST YOU?

Among the sayings of Jesus recorded in Luke's Gospel, there is one on faithfulness that runs counter to the common wisdom of our day, as popularized by Richard Carlson's 1990s blockbuster *Don't Sweat the Small Stuff . . . and It's All Small Stuff*.[10] In a piece of contrarian wisdom Jesus says, "Whoever is faithful in a very little is faithful also in much; and whoever is dishonest in a very little is dishonest also in much. If then you have not been faithful with the dishonest wealth, who will entrust to you the true riches?" (Luke 16:10-11). Unfortunately, when it comes to diversity leadership, Jesus has it all over Carlson: sweat the small stuff . . . and it's all small stuff. Trust is eroded by the cumulative effect of small abrasions caused by leaders' inadvertent insensitivities. A single grain of sand is endurable, but when single grains are aggregated, as in sandpaper, the effect is wearing.

Building trust requires leaders to *put diversity leadership into practice whenever possible*. Put in the light of Jesus' instruction in Luke 16:10-11, trust-building is an exercise in practicing in small things the kinds of attitudes, perceptions, and behaviors that leaders in the church must be prepared to exhibit when a large challenge arises. Effective diversity leadership is not a flotation device or an emergency preparedness plan to be activated only in a crisis. Instead, it is the habitual cultivation even in "the small stuff" of the attitudes, perceptions, and behaviors that together constitute diversity expertise. If we wait until a crisis arises, we are out of time to practice and it is too late to prepare our congregation and ourselves to weather the storm.

Two days before a presidential campaign fundraiser, the

state campaign chair and two aides were going over last-minute details. A young national campaign staffer walked in, looking at his PDA.

"What do you know about your senior pastor?" the staffer asked the campaign chair.

"I know he's my pastor," he responded. "Why?"

"Are you aware that he preached against the war in Iraq?" the staffer inquired.

"I was there for that sermon," the chair replied. The staffer looked again at the device in his hand.

"Are you aware that he publicly attacked the new national security strategy?" the staffer continued.

"I was there for that sermon, too," the chair responded.

"Well, we don't think he should be on the program," said the staffer.

"Are you telling me you think I should call my pastor and uninvite him?" asked the chair.

"What I'm saying is we don't think he should be on the program."

The chair paused for a moment and then said, "He's my pastor. I invited him, and he'll be on the program."

The chair, appointed after the election to serve as a U.S. ambassador, could have called his pastor and leveled with him: there are people in the national campaign who object to your being on the program because of public positions you have taken. His pastor would have understood. In fact, when the chair first invited him, the pastor had suggested that there were other pastors in the area—even on his own staff—who might be better candidates to give the invocation for the one-thousand-dollars-a-plate fundraiser.

"No," the chair had insisted. "You are my pastor. I want you to do it."

"Then I'd be honored," the pastor responded. And he was. The chair had a lot riding on this event, and he certainly didn't need a problem with the national campaign staff. But he chose to stand by his pastor with whom he disagreed, even when his own reputation and aspirations were on the line. And when he did, he exemplified diversity leadership in politics and in the church by responding in the same way that he had practiced for decades. Standing by one another and standing up for one another even when we disagree with one another must be practiced regularly in small things to build the trust that is indispensable for leaders and congregations alike to be prepared to exhibit diversity maturity when larger challenges arise.

WHAT ARE YOU DOING HERE?

After Elijah's massacre of the four hundred fifty prophets of Baal in the Wadi Kishon following his triumph in the contest on Mount Carmel in 1 Kings 18:20-40, Queen Jezebel swore out a death threat against him. In response, Elijah fled "into the wilderness . . . forty days and forty nights to Horeb the mount of God." Discouraged and depressed, "He came to a cave, and spent the night there" (19:4-9) in a full-fledged "retreat." Caught in a vicious cycle of increasingly violent conflict in which he was as much a perpetrator as a victim, Elijah ran away. But he could not escape the divine questioning. An identical inquiry comes twice to Elijah: "What are you doing here?" (19:9, 13).

In our time, as in Elijah's, the cultural climate is ripe for diversity whiplash: "success," however it may be defined, brings new threats as assuredly as it provides new opportunities. The apostle Paul, well acquainted with diversity-driven conflict, commented, "A wide door for effective work has opened to me, *and* [not "but"] there are many adversaries" (1 Corinthians 16:9, emphasis added). Indeed, when it comes to diversity leadership, the most important and effective work is always done in contexts of resistance and conflict rather than in settings of acquiescence and acceptance. When change agents and leaders find themselves "preaching to the choir," they can be sure that they are not engaged in diversity leadership. On Mount Horeb, Elijah bemoaned the fact that he had no choir to whom to preach. God's response was to send Elijah back into the conflict.

Asking ourselves the divine question, "What are you doing here?" reminds us of the importance of our own mission and vision in diversity leadership.

One weekday evening in the aftermath of a congregational crisis over sexual orientation and denominational politics, three men in their late forties, who had played disparate but indispensable roles in the effort to see the congregation through the conflict, found themselves by happenstance—or perhaps by providence—together in an otherwise empty conference room. In a few quiet moments of commiseration, they expressed their respective surprise that over the previous months they had each been supporting a position that was not their own but which they believed was the wisest and best course of action for their church at that particular time. "Sometimes," said one of them, "I ask myself what in the world I am doing here." After a poignant and pregnant silence, one of them said quietly, "We are here for this. Who else but us? Where else but here?" Diversity leadership requires a sense of mission—why we are here—and a vision—what we are working toward—on the part of individual leaders before clarity of vision and a commitment to mission can become an integral part of the congregational culture.

Before congregations can engage effectively in *reviewing priorities and devising a plan* for dealing with diversity, individual congregational leaders must blaze the trail by doing the same. Because even so-called "homogeneous" congregations include a challenging array of diversities—including faith development, gender, personality type, spiritual type, and many others—it is impossible to engage diversity battles on every possible front. Prioritizing is necessary. Planning is indispensable. The good news is that by engaging diversity effectively on only one or a few fronts, individuals and congregations can begin to enhance their diversity maturity and expand their diversity expertise overall because this maturity and expertise is eminently transferable. Again, cultivating diversity expertise in a very little builds trust in much.

One way to take this next step in diversity leadership—reviewing priorities and devising a plan—is to return to the biblical responses to diversity that we identified above as our "typical" response and draw a line from it to a response that we might need to develop to become more effective in our diversity leadership. For example, if I have identified myself as a "coexister," I might set as a goal for myself to become more "conversational" in my encounter with people with perspectives, attitudes, or behaviors different from my own. Again, as Donald Phillip Verene has insisted, putting questions rather than engaging in arguments moves us forward in our self-understanding and in our understanding of others. Instead of saying, "Well, I disagree, but you know what they say: 'different strokes for different folks,'" and walking away, we might now respond, "Really? I don't usually look at it that way. Tell me why you do." Or, if I am a collaborationist, I might take the time to identify the gaps in the variety of those persons with whom I tend to collaborate: "Who am I still missing or avoiding in the work I do?" Some of us might discover that we collaborate quite well with diversity to the left of us, but not so well to the right of us, or vice versa.

Alternatively, if the self-examination at the beginning of this chapter identified certain attributes, perceptions, attitudes, or behaviors that are difficult for us to accept, work with, or learn from, we can set out to explore our ability to live and work across our own discomforting lines. A senior pastor was both gratified and challenged when a same-sex couple in a long-term relationship joined the congregation he served. He took it as a sign of the congregation's hospitality and welcome that the two women felt comfortable enough to make this congregation their church home for themselves and the two children they were rearing together. But he also knew that "groundbreaking" couples face peculiar pressures and tensions in congregations, and this was uncharted territory for this church and this couple—and this pastor. One of his responses was to move into uncharted territory himself by becoming a patient of the partner in this relationship who was a physician. If he was going to expect members of the congregation to step across long-held lines of demarcation, then he was going to have to model the same behavior himself. When a disconcerted member approached him one day and asked, "What do you know about this couple?" he responded, "Well, Evelyn's my doctor, and she's a very good one." The tone of the conversation changed dramatically.

Reviewing priorities and devising a plan—setting goals and objectives and developing concrete steps that lead to accomplishing those objectives and goals—is indispensable behavior for individuals as well as congregations in the cultivation of wise and effective diversity leadership. It is only when we ourselves are traveling the road—or scaling the mountain—that we can lead others along the way. "Sometimes I ask myself what in the world I am doing here," indeed. "We are here for this. Who else but us? Where else but here?"

PAUL THE PRACTITIONER: MISSION, VISION, AND STRATEGY

A Sermon on Romans 12:1-8

Back when I was still a professor of religion instead of a mere practitioner of it, I was a proponent of a school of interpretation that has said since the nineteenth century that Paul's "main argument" in his letter to the church at Rome is already over by the time we get to the verses in front of us, Romans 12:1-8. Regular churchgoers wouldn't be surprised to hear such a thing. It's not unusual for a congregation to recognize that a sermon has hit the skids long before the preacher stops talking. So scholars and churchgoers alike can agree that it makes sense that the argument in Romans might very well be over well before Paul's letter ends.

But now that I am a practitioner instead of a professor, I subscribe to an entirely different school of interpretation. It's a school that emulates that most inimitable of all interpreters, the greatest of all American Yogis, a teacher of amazing and confounding expression, the venerable Yogi Berra, who summed up his interpretive method in the memorable phrase, "It ain't over 'til it's over." According to the Yogi Berra school of interpretation, if Paul's main argument had been over in Romans 8 or Romans 11, as many scholars have suggested, he would have stopped. But it wasn't, and he didn't, because Paul was not merely a professor of religion; he was a practitioner also. The argument in his letter to the church in Rome could not be over until he had addressed how the great theological ideas in chapters 1–11 were to be translated into great and faithful living. So beginning in Romans 12, Paul moves from talking about great ideas to talking about great living.

Paul begins Romans 12 by proposing a peculiar mission for the Christian life. According to Paul in verse 1, the essence of the Christian mission is sacrificial living. "I appeal to you," Paul says, "to present your bodies as a living sacrifice, holy and acceptable to God, which is your spiritual worship." Paul grounds the mission of the Christian life in the language of worship and sacrifice familiar to his audience from the Jewish and pagan ritual systems of the Greco-Roman world. When we are "called to belong to Jesus Christ" (1:6), Paul says, our mission is to lay our selves on the altar to God (12:1). There is something of a double entendre at the end of verse 1 because the Greek word that is translated "worship" also means "service." Spelled out, then, the mission of the Christian life is sacrificial living in the service of God, which in itself is an act of worship.

There is nothing easy about that mission, then or now. Paul knew that. In fact, if we had been reading Romans in the language in which it was composed, we might have recognized the challenge ahead of us from the first word of chapter 12. When Paul says, "I appeal to you," he borrowed a word that "was used in classical Gr[eek] of exhorting troops who were about to go into battle."[1] So, when Paul turns his attention from the profession of great theological ideas to the practice of great and faithful living, his very first word has a military lineage. Whenever and wherever we find our best efforts at faithful Christian living to be a struggle or a conflict-riddled enterprise, we should not be surprised or disheartened or discouraged, because that's exactly how the apostle Paul characterized it at the beginning of Romans 12. To be sure, if we are honest with ourselves, most of us would have to admit that we are at best weekend warriors (and occasionally on Wednesday evenings). We may give up a little something for Lent, but giving up our whole self as a living sacrifice in the service of God that may turn out to be more like armed conflict than a lovefeast is a whole lot more than most of us want to offer. There are, of course, always those Christians who see the military imagery here and elsewhere in the New Testament and teach and preach as though faithful Christian living is about taking up arms and conquering everyone who disagrees with you or is different from you. But in Romans 8:37, Paul expressly said that those who belong to Jesus Christ are not conquerors but "are more than conquerors." And in Romans 12:1 he spells it out: we become "more than conquerors" through sacrificial living in the service of God. That's the mission that Paul lays claim to in Romans 12:1.

In verse 2, Paul moves from mission to vision. Paul articulates a dynamic and fluid vision of a faithful community and faithful individuals who are constantly being renewed, reformed, and transformed even. Paul writes: "Do not be conformed to this world, but be transformed by the renewing of your minds, so that you may discern what is the will of God—what is good and acceptable and perfect." Paul's vision of the Christian life and of Christian community is of a work forever in progress. Would that we could ever say that it is finished. Would that we could say, "Here it is. We have done it. We have created the perfect expression of the Christian life and the Christian community in this time and place for all times and all places." But replacing the Christian journey with a Christian destination would be the worst thing that could happen to us. Once we arrived at that perfect expression of Christian faith and practice, you and I would set about forcing it on everyone else in the church and around the world. We would turn our take on the gospel into a Christian law that governs the public and private lives of everyone. We would shift our vision from transforming to conforming, and that's precisely what Paul says not to do: "Do not be conformed" to this world's status quo, even if it is a status quo of our own making.

For some of us, the challenge presented by Paul's vision is to let go of the status quo that we have worked so hard to achieve and to maintain. We don't want renewal or reform, and certainly not transformation. We like things just the way they are, thank you very much. As far as we're concerned, what is "good and acceptable and perfect" already exists right here, right now—or at least close enough to it for us. Don't change a thing. For others of us, the challenge is to give up our perversion of Paul's vision in which we take it upon ourselves to forcibly reform or transform the church and the world. We set ourselves up as agents of divinely authorized change, and we insist that transformation and reformation is what others must do to conform to our "good and acceptable and perfect" intent. More often than not, defenders of the status quo on one side and agents of forced reform on the other side both twist the model prayer from "Thy kingdom come, thy will be done" into "Our kingdom come, our will be done." But Paul proposes a dynamic and fluid vision of the constant transforming, reforming, and renewing of our minds—not "others' minds," mind you—in order for us to discern the "good and acceptable and perfect" intent of God for us all "on earth as it is in heaven." According to Paul's vision in Romans 12:2, the church is always under construction; always undergoing renovation, reformation, and transformation. As individuals and as a community, we are forever a work in progress.

Now, if Paul had been a professor of religion, he could have stopped right there with mission and vision—and left the rest to the mere practitioners. But Paul was a practitioner as well as a professor of his faith, so he recognized that it would be a pointless academic exercise to put forward a mission and articulate a vision without identifying strategies that would move individuals and communities toward living into the vision and living out the mission. So in Romans 12:3-8, Paul moves from mission and vision to two indispensable strategies for great and faithful living.

Paul's first strategy for great and faithful living is an unlikely and counterintuitive starting point, then and now: "I say to everyone among you," Paul writes, "not to think of yourself more highly than you ought to think" (v. 3). Living out the mission and living into the vision of the Christian life begins with—of all things—humility. In a culture like ours that worships achievement, stardom, and attention getting, humility seems like an odd opening strategy for great living. Perhaps we should be reminded of Jesus' assertion that "whoever wants to be first must be last of all and servant of all" (Mark 9:35). Humility above all else was found in Christ, according to the early Christian hymn that Paul quotes in Philippians:

> Christ Jesus, who, though he was in the form of God,
>   did not regard equality with God
>   as something to be exploited,
> but emptied himself,
>   taking the form of a slave,
>   being born in human likeness.
> And being found in human form,
>   he humbled himself
>   and became obedient to point of death—
> even death on a cross. (Philippians 2:5-8)

Christ, then, epitomized humility in sacrificial living in the service of God. Paul writes: "Do nothing from selfish ambition or conceit, but in humility regard others as better than yourselves. Let each of you look not to your own interests, but to the interests of others" (Philippians 2:3-4).

Now, I've been around long enough to know that some of us will be quick to dismiss this humility stuff as the very worst in Milquetoast theology. You know, the sort of thing that sounds good in church on Sunday but will never fly in the real world the other six days. So for those of us who think that Jesus and Paul are yapping up the wrong sapling, I want us to consider for a moment what Jim Collins and his management research team discovered in the analysis that led to the publication of the business blockbuster *Good to Great: Why Some Companies Make the Leap . . . and Others Don't.* Collins and his team of researchers identified eleven good-to-great companies that distinguished themselves from the rest of their Fortune 500 cohort by moving from mediocrity to greatness and sustaining that greatness for at least fifteen years. One of the common denominators in these good-to-great cases was a leader—a CEO, mind you—who was characterized by words like "quiet, humble, modest, reserved, shy, gracious, mild-mannered, self-effacing, understated, did not believe his own clippings; and so forth."[2] These surprising characteristics of the breakthrough executives who brought a "ferocious resolve" to turning mediocre companies into great ones were so remarkable to the research team that they initially "penciled in terms like 'selfless executive' and 'servant leader'" to describe these CEOs.[3] And in a remarkable contrast, Collins writes, "In over two-thirds of the comparison cases, we noted the presence of a gargantuan personal ego that contributed to the demise or continued mediocrity of the company."[4]

As unlikely and counterintuitive as it may be to us, humility is a strategic starting point for greatness—in corporate leadership and Christian living alike. Arrogance and conceit, self-interest and self-aggrandizement are consistent not with greatness but with mediocrity, and they are fundamentally incompatible with Paul's vision of constant renewal and his mission of sacrificial living.

Paul's second indispensable strategy for great and faithful living involves rightly discerning the nature of unity and diversity in the church. Paul says, "For as in one body we have many members, and not all the members have the same function, so we, who are many, are one body in Christ, and individually we are members one of another" (Romans 12:4).

Notice, first, not what Paul says but how he says it. In verse 3, Paul put forward an appeal for humility. An exhortation. An argument, if you will. But in verses 4-6, he neither appeals for unity nor argues for diversity. In Paul's way of thinking about the church, both the unity in "one body" and the diversity of "many members" are givens, not goals or aspirations, appeals or arguments. Diversity is a sociological given in the church, not a theological project. Unity is a theological given in the church, not a political enterprise. Diversity comes with the territory of human congregation, and unity comes with the territory of being individually and together "in Christ." Like it or not, believe it or not, understand it or not, accept it or not, those who "belong to Jesus Christ" (1:6) are already together as "one body" and already individually "members one of another" (12:5). Notice, second, that Paul is clear about the differences that make a strategic difference in the one body: "We have gifts that differ" (v. 6), and "not all the members have the same function" (v. 4). Paul's silence is as telling as his words. Paul does not mention attributes and traits. Paul says nothing about identities and ideologies. Hot-button diversity issues of Paul's time and ours go entirely unmentioned at the strategic level of discourse. The differences that make a strategic difference in the community are gifts and functions, not attributes and identities. The more we obsess and quarrel over the latter, the farther we fall from Paul's mission, vision, and strategy for Christian living, individually and in community; but the more that we cultivate and clarify the former—our gifts and functions—the stronger the body grows and the healthier its members become.

To return to Paul's metaphor of the sacrificial system with which he began in Romans 12:1, some of us are sheep and some of us are goats (Leviticus 1:10). Some of us are turtledoves and some are pigeons (Leviticus 1:14). Some of us are oxen and some of us are lambs (Leviticus 17:3). And some of us are sumptuously fatted calves (Leviticus 9:2-3). And for all our differences and disagreements—some of them so obvious and some so deep that we appear to one another as of different species altogether, still we are in Christ one body called together and individually in humility and in unity and in diversity to a vision of constant transformation and renewal and to a mission of sacrificial living in the service of God "from whom and through whom and to whom are all things; to whom be the glory forever. Amen" (Romans 11:36, adapted).

NOTES

1. A Diverse New World—and Old

1. Lyle E. Schaller, *The New Context for Ministry: Competing for the Charitable Dollar* (Nashville: Abingdon Press, 2002), 231.

2. Schaller puts the question directly: "How Costly Is Diversity?" He concludes, "Demographic diversity and/or theological pluralism usually costs money! Homogeneity costs less than heterogeneity in building a constituency" (ibid.).

3. Best described in Diana L. Eck, *Encountering God: The Spiritual Journey from Bozeman to Banaras*, rev. ed. (Boston: Beacon Press, 2003), 166-99. Briefly stated, the exclusivist perspective contends, "Our own community, our tradition, our understanding of reality, our encounter with God, is the one and only truth, excluding all others" (p. 168). The pluralist viewpoint asserts, "Truth is not the exclusive or inclusive possession of any one tradition or community. Therefore the diversity of communities, traditions, understandings of the truth, and visions of God is not an obstacle for us to overcome, but an opportunity for our energetic engagement and dialogue with one another" (p. 168).

4. Cassandra King, *The Sunday Wife* (New York: Hyperion, 2002), 66-67.

5. R. Roosevelt Thomas Jr., *Beyond Race and Gender: Unleashing the Power of Your Total Work Force by Managing Diversity* (New York: AMACOM, 1991), 3.

6. Ibid., 2.

7. Wade Clark Roof and William McKinney, *American Mainline Religion: Its Changing Shape and Future* (New Brunswick, NJ: Rutgers University Press, 1987), 249.

8. Jackson W. Carroll and Wade Clark Roof, *Bridging Divided Worlds: Generational Cultures in Congregations* (San Francisco: Jossey-Bass, 2002), 11.

9. Robert Wuthnow, *After Heaven: Spirituality in America Since the 1950s* (Berkeley: University of California Press, 1998). More recently, Wuthnow has documented and analyzed "how we as individuals and as a nation are responding to the challenges of increasing religious and cultural diversity" in *America and the Challenges of Religious Diversity* (Princeton, NJ: Princeton University Press, 2005, xi.).

10. William Sloane Coffin, *A Passion for the Possible: A Message to U.S. Churches* (Louisville: Westminister John Knox Press, 1993), 7-8.

11. Abraham ben Isaiah and Benjamin Sharfman, eds., *The Pentateuch and Rashi's Commentary: A Linear Translation into English* (Brooklyn: S. S. & R. Publishing, 1976), I.40. Emphasis added.

12. Jaroslav Pelikan, ed., *Luther's Works* (St. Louis: Concordia, 1958), I.257.

13. Charles Kimball, *When Religion Becomes Evil* (San Francisco: HarperSanFrancisco, 2002), 4.

14. Ibid., 16-17.

15. Martin E. Marty, *When Faiths Collide* (Malden, MA: Blackwell Publishing, 2005.

16. Diana L. Eck, *A New Religious America: How a "Christian Country" Has Now Become the World's Most Religiously Diverse Nation* (San Francisco: HarperSanFrancisco, 2001), 4.

17. Ibid., 3, 4-5.

18. Eck goes on to insist that the issue be framed in terms of *pluralism*, which she defines as "the dynamic process through which we engage with one another in and through our very deepest differences" (ibid., 70). Eck is a pioneer and perfecter of the pluralistic enterprise, and she has expertly modeled the move from personal conviction to dispassionate observation to authentic engagement. At the same time, not everyone in local congregations is capable of going directly from Bozeman to Banaras as she did, making the leap of interfaith onto the intellectual and spiritual trail that she has blazed straight up the mountain. Others will require a gentler grade, replete with the switchbacks, overlooks, and rest areas that this treatment attempts to carve out by introducing congregational leaders to a new definition of diversity and the cultivation of more effective responses to diversity in the church. By whatever terminology and line of approach we use, we are both committed to "the dynamic process through which we engage with one another in and through our very deepest differences."

19. John P. Kotter, *Leading Change* (Boston: Harvard Business School Press, 1996), 68.

20. Walter Brueggemann, *The Prophetic Imagination* (Philadelphia: Fortress Press, 1978), 11.

21. Ibid., 24-25.

22. Donald Phillip Verene, *The Art of Humane Education* (Ithaca, NY: Cornell University Press, 2002), 2-3.

23. Ibid., 3 (emphasis added).

24. R. Roosevelt Thomas Jr. with Marjorie I. Woodruff, *Building a House for Diversity: How a Fable About a Giraffe and an Elephant Offers New Strategies for Today's Workforce* (New York: AMACOM, 1999), 5.

25. Ibid., 16.

26. Ibid., 15.

27. Ibid., 5 (emphasis added).

28. Verene, *The Art of Humane Education*, 11.

29. Ibid., 11-12.

30. Thomas, *Building a House*, 14-15.

31. The language of "ultimate concern" is from Paul Tillich, *Systematic Theology*, vol. 1, *Reason and Revelation, Being and God* (Chicago: University of Chicago Press, 1951), 12. Diversity is not an "ultimate concern"; it is merely a "preliminary concern," using Tillich's distinction. Still, according to Tillich, "In and through every preliminary concern the ultimate concern can actualize itself" (p. 13).

32. Eck, *Encountering God*, 97.

33. Jürgen Moltmann, *The Trinity and The Kingdom* (San Francisco: Harper & Row, 1981), 198, 199.

34. http://amsterdam.park.org/Guests/Russia/moscow/sergiev/rublev.html; accessed June 3, 2005.

35. Ibid.

Sermon: Straddling the Fence—or Leaping It

This sermon was originally delivered in the closing worship service of the Gardner-Webb University Faculty Retreat at Ridgecrest Conference Center, Black Mountain, NC, August 18, 2004.

1. Reading verse 6 with 1QIsaᵃ, the so-called "great Isaiah scroll" from Cave 1 at Qumran.

2. Donald Phillip Verene, *The Art of Humane Education* (Ithaca, NY: Cornell University Press, 2002), 11.

3. Ibid., 11-12.

4. Elizabeth Barrett Browning, "How Do I Love Thee?" in *Immortal Poems of the English Language: British and American Poetry from Chaucer's Time to the Present Day*, ed. Oscar Williams (New York: Pocket Books, 1973), 349.

2. Biblical Responses to Diversity: Conquest, Coexistence, and Coercion

1. On calling down a consuming fire on one's opponents as a prophetic action, see Elijah's behavior in 2 Kings 1:9-14.

2. See the discussion and bibliography cited in "Slavery," *The Anchor Bible Dictionary* (New York: Doubleday, 1992).

Sermon: So Far As It Depends on You

This sermon is adapted from sermons originally delivered at First Baptist Church, Greenville, SC, on September 16, September 23, and November 18, 2001.

1. Reading with NRSV footnote n.

2. Thomas Merton, trans., *The Wisdom of the Desert: Sayings from the Desert Fathers of the Fourth Century* (Boston: Shambhala, 2004), 68.

3. Biblical Responses to Diversity: Conversion, Compassionate Action, and Conversation

1. Rashi, "Genesis," in *The Pentateuch and Rashi's Commentary: A Linear Translation into English*, vol. 1, *Genesis*, ed. Abraham ben Isaiah and Benjamin Scharfman (Brooklyn: S. S. & R. Publishing, 1976), 31; emphasis added.

2. Ibid.

3. Ibid., 39. The received Hebrew text lacks the content of what Cain "said" to Abel, "Let us go out to the field," which NRSV and most other modern translations supply on the basis of the Samaritan Pentateuch and the Septuagint.

Sermon: Like a Child

This sermon was delivered at Faith Memorial Chapel in Cedar Mountain, NC, on August 20, 2006. It is adapted from a sermon delivered at First Baptist Church, Greenville, SC, on July 8, 2001.

4. Biblical Responses to Diversity: Collaboration

1. For a helpful overview, see Richard J. Clifford, "Introduction to Wisdom Literature," in *The New Interpreter's Bible*, vol. 5 (Nashville: Abingdon Press, 1997), 1-16.

2. Ibid., 7.

3. James B. Pritchard, *Ancient Near Eastern Texts Relating to the Old Testament*, 2nd ed. (Princeton, NJ: Princeton University Press, 1955), 427.

4. Ibid., 424.

5. Ibid., 422.

6. Ibid., 423.

7. See, similarly, Proverbs 1:29; 2:5; 3:7; 9:10; 15:33; 19:23; 31:30; and Job 28:28.

8. Isaiah 29:14 in 1 Corinthians 1:19; Jeremiah 9:24 in 1:31; Isaiah 64:4 (perhaps) in 2:9; and Isaiah 40:13 in 2:16 (at the close of his treatment, he finally quotes wisdom literature, Job 5:12-13, as well as Psalm 94:11, in 1 Corinthians 3:19-20).

9. Richard B. Hays, *1 Corinthians*, in *Interpretation: A Bible Commentary for Teaching and Preaching* (Louisville: John Knox Press, 1997), 43. Similarly, Matthew 11:25-26 recounts, "At that time Jesus said, 'I thank you, Father, Lord of heaven and earth, because you have hidden these things from the wise and the intelligent and have revealed them to infants; yes, Father, for such was your gracious will.'"

10. For an introduction to apocalyptic thought and literature see the five brief articles collected under the entry "Apocalypses and Apocalypticism," in *The Anchor Bible Dictionary*, vol. 1 (New York: Doubleday, 1992), 279-92.

Sermon: The Narrow Gate

This sermon is an adaptation of the keynote address for the First Annual Community Thanksgiving Celebration of Greenville Faith Communities United, November 18, 2004, at Springfield Baptist Church, Dr. John Corbitt, pastor. An excerpt from it appeared as "Build bridges from the middle: History of Thanksgiving shows need for conversation, collaboration" in the *Charlotte (NC) Observer* (November 18, 2006), page 3E.

1. William Butler Yeats, "The Second Coming," in *The Norton Anthology of Poetry*, rev. ed., ed. Alexander W. Allison et al. (New York: W. W. Norton & Company, 1975), 923.

2. Martin E. Marty, "The Hard Middle," in *Sightings*, March 1, 2004; http://marty-center.uchicago.edu/sightings/archive_/2004/0301.shtml.

5. Diversity Leadership: Questions of Culture

1. Donald Phillip Verene, *The Art of Humane Education* (Ithaca, NY: Cornell University Press, 2002), pp. 2-3.

2. R. Roosevelt Thomas Jr. with Marjorie I. Woodruff, *Building a House for Diversity: How a Fable About a Giraffe and an Elephant Offers New Strategies for Today's Workforce* (New York: AMACOM, 1999), 213.

3. Ibid., 212.

4. R. Roosevelt Thomas Jr., *Beyond Race and Gender: Unleashing the Power of Your Total Work Force by Managing Diversity* (New York: AMACOM, 1991), 53.

5. Ibid., 52.

6. Ibid. The reader is reminded of the reassessment of Jesus' words about "like a child" in the sermon "Nails and Gold and Everything Bold," above.

7. Even though the distinctive familial terminology such as *genos* (family, descendants, relatives), *patria* (family, clan, lineage), *syggenēs* or *syggeneia* (kindred, relatives), and *phylē* (tribe) can be applied more broadly than to family in the narrow sense of the sociological unit, the New Testament writings do not apply these terms to the church, with the exception of 1 Peter 2:9, which appears to be drawing on Isaiah 43:20, "chosen people," and James 1:1 in which the faithful are allegorically referred to as "the twelve tribes in the Dispersion."

8. C. S. Lewis, *Mere Christianity* (New York: Macmillan, 1952), 159.

9. Hans Conzelmann, *Acts of the Apostles; Hermeneia—A Critical and Historical Commentary on the Bible* (Philadelphia: Fortress Press, 1987), 71.

10. Thomas, *Building a House*, 55.

11. Lyle E. Schaller, *The New Context for Ministry: Competing for the Charitable Dollar* (Nashville: Abingdon Press, 2002), 228.

12. Ibid.

13. Ibid., 229.

14. Ibid., 229-30.

15. William T. Cavanaugh, "Is Public Theology Really Public? Some Problems with Civil Society," *Annual of the Society of Christian Ethics* 21 (2001): 117. Cavanaugh goes on to point out that as "church," the New Testament *ekklēsia* was made up even of those who were "by definition excluded from being citizens" of the Greek city-state: "women, children, slaves—are given full membership through baptism."

16. *The Art of Humane Education*, 2-3.

17. Thomas, *Building a House*, 216.

18. Ibid., 215.

19. Ibid., 17, emphasis added.

20. Ibid.

Sermon: The Mission-First Jesus

This sermon originally appeared in the Winter 2006 issue of *Review and Expositor*, dedicated to Jewish-Baptist dialogue and edited by Daniel Goodman, under the title "Texts of Terror and the Essence of Scripture: Encountering the Jesus of John 8." *Review and Expositor* 103, no. 1 (Winter 2006).

1. Rudolph Bultmann, *The Gospel of John: A Commentary*, trans. G. R. Beasley-Murray et al. (Philadelphia: Westminster, 1971), 314.

6. Diversity Leadership: Questions of the Individual Journey

1. R. Roosevelt Thomas Jr. with Marjorie I. Woodruff, *Building a House for Diversity: How a Fable About a Giraffe and an Elephant Offers New Strategies for Today's Workforce* (New York: AMACOM, 1999), 213.

2. Ibid., 62.

3. Ibid., 203.

4. Ibid., 203-10.

5. Rashi writes on Genesis 3:9 that God "knew where he was but [He asked where Adam was] to enter into conversation with him so that he should not be afraid to answer. . . . So [in the case of] Cain (Gen 4:9)," where the commentary reads, "To enter with him into words of gentleness, perhaps he would repent." *The Pentateuch and Rashi's Commentary: A Linear Translation into English*, vol. 1, *Genesis*, ed. Abraham ben Isaiah and Benjamin Scharfman (Brooklyn: S. S. & R. Publishing, 1976), 31, 39.

6. *Building a House*, 203.

7. Ibid., 16. See discussion above in chapter 1, pages 13-14.

8. Ibid., 5.

9. Ibid., 16.

10. Richard Carlson, *Don't Sweat the Small Stuff . . . and It's All Small Stuff: Simple Ways to Keep the Little Things from Taking Over Your Life* (New York: Hyperion, 1997).

Sermon: Paul the Practitioner: Mission, Vision, and Strategy

This sermon is adapted from a Lenten Meditation delivered at Christ Church Episcopal, Greenville, SC, on March 22, 2006, Dr. Bob Dannals, Rector.

1. Fritz Reineker, *A Linguistic Key to the Greek New Testament*, vol. 2 (Grand Rapids: Zondervan, 1980), 29.

2. Jim Collins, *Good to Great: Why Some Companies Make the Leap . . . and Others Don't* (New York: HarperBusiness, 2001), 27.

3. Ibid., 30.

4. Ibid., 29.